Return to Bedrock

Beyond the Layers of Tradition

Dean Youngsma

Revival Quest Publications

Unless otherwise stated, all Scripture quotations are taken from *The New American Standard Bible (NAS)©* 1960, 1962, 1968, 1971, 1975, 1977 by The Lockman Foundation. Used by permission. Or, *The Holy Bible, New International Version* © 1978 by The International Bible Society. Used by permission of Zondervan Bible Publisher.

All Scripture has been italicized for identification and emphasis.

RETURN TO BEDROCK *Second Edition*
First Edition released under the title: *Bedrock Christianity*
Dean Youngsma
Revival Quest Publishing
P.O. Box 62
Fortuna, CA 95540

ISBN: 0-9678667-2-3
Library of Congress Catalog Card Number: 2004095657
Printed in the United States of America
Copyright © 2004 Dean Youngsma

No part of this book may be reproduced or transmitted in any form or by any means, electronic or mechanical, including photocopying, recording, or by any information storage and retrieval system, without permission in writing from the author and publisher.

Cover Design: Alan Olmstead / Sirius Studios, Eureka, CA

TABLE OF CONTENTS

Preface.. 5

1 Bedrock Christianity..7

2 Riding the White Horse – Truth...................... 15

3 The History Lesson.. 25

4 Double Vision..37

5 Tensions of Revelation......................................49

6 Free at Last..63

7 Religious Conflict...79

8 Trouble in River City...97

9 The Journey of Life in the Kingdom................107

10 The Goat and the Tire......................................125

11 The Kingdom of Love...135

My Legacy..149

PREFACE

This newly titled second edition is a redo of my first book, *Bedrock Christianity*. In this edition I have tightened the text, changed the format, and clarified and edited some of the content. I also reorganized, condensed, and moved chapters to enhance readability.

Return to Bedrock is an exhortation to go back to the simple foundations of early Christianity. Bedrock is the solid layer underlying all soil, sand, gravel, and loose material on the earth's surface, which lies beneath the superficial rock. Bedrock is the lowest or very bottom level, a secure foundation. It is the fundamental basic principles or facts. Throughout the Old Covenant, Jesus is referred to as the Rock and the Redeemer. It is this Rock (the Messiah of our salvation) on which the river of God flows.

Do you not sometimes fantasize about what it was like to live in the early days of the Christian era? I do. My heart yearns for the days of simplicity, purity, passion, and zeal. Where are the zealots of our day? Perhaps you are, or will be, one of them.

God led the children of Israel out of Egypt and out of the house of bondage. Christ died to set the captives free. Freedom is what God wants for his people. Any person, place, or thing that steals that freedom is the spirit of the antichrist. Many believers in Christ choose to live in Egypt, the place of bondage. God has a purpose and plan for you and it is not Egypt.

I

Bedrock Christianity

"Trust in the Lord forever, for in God the Lord, we have an everlasting Rock" (Isaiah 26:4).

Life is a journey and not an event. Every person should be on a lifelong quest to know God better. One's goal in life should not be to seek personal happiness, but peace with God. Some of this book is about my journey in God and some of the things I've learned along the way.

In the spring of 1998, my wife and I were holding revival meetings at various locations throughout Humboldt County, California. We constantly sought the Lord about where He wanted us to meet. We then telephoned the people who liked to attend these gatherings to notify them of our location for that particular week. We held these meetings every Friday night for about six months.

On Wednesday, May 1, the Lord put it into my mind to have a special sunset service at Moonstone Beach, located between Arcata and Trinidad on the North Coast. As we headed north that Wednesday (to secure permission for our service), I "blew the engine" in our 1985 Buick, our only car. We drove it into Eureka to a towing company. (The owner and his wife had helped us with music in previous revival meetings.) He told me that our vehicle dropped in value from $5,000 to $300. He said, "Why don't you take that 1986 Lincoln Continental over there and drive it until we can figure out what to do."

Our trip to Moonstone had been delayed for less than an hour. On our way again, we secured the location for the beach service.

That particular Wednesday was a white puffy cloud day and I had visions of it being the same on Friday. However, on Wednesday night it began to rain, and it rained all day and all night Thursday and all day Friday. A few people called to see if we were still having the service. Since God was in control, I answered in the affirmative. The Lord put it into my mind to have this sunset gathering and if it was raining, He had a purpose in that, too.

Even as we headed to the beach, it was raining. When we arrived to set up at about 6:00 p.m., the rain diminished to a misty drizzle and within a half hour it stopped completely. We started a large bonfire to warm ourselves. As the people began to show up, they were amazed how the rain had stopped just in time for the service. The Lord had been teaching us all to listen to His voice and not look at the circumstances. I believe God was testing our faithfulness that day.

The interesting thing about all this is that we could look to the town of Trinidad a few miles to the north and see that it was raining there; then look to the south a few miles and see that it was also raining in Arcata. We could look straight overhead and see the moon and patchy blue-gray skies. We were all overcome with the awesome power of God in the situation. He was delighted with us and we were delighted with God.

As the sun began to set, the sky turned to gold. The waves danced and shimmered beautiful golden colors. It looked like a thousand angels singing to the glory of God in the highest. The joy we all felt was inexpressible. The moon was bright and full and provided the extra light needed for our time of celebration.

We had a great time of fellowship and singing around the bonfire. I gave a short message and each person shared a brief testimony about how they came to know the Lord. Each one of us then lit a stick and then threw it into the fire, symbolizing our individual light and how it becomes brighter when we are united in Christ.

At about 10:30 p.m., a large wave came within several yards of our meeting; it was like the Lord was saying that this was the time to pack-up and go home.

I will never forget that night, because God showed up in great His power. He set the table and we dined in His presence. It did not take an earthquake or a tsunami to experience His power. All it took was obedience.

Now let me tell you the rest of the story about the Lincoln Continental we borrowed. We kept the car over the weekend, planning to return it on Monday afternoon. Monday morning I was scheduled to speak to the seniors' group at a church in Eureka. We shared our vision for ministry, and they gave us a $203 offering.

After the meeting, we went to the towing company to see if we could purchase the Lincoln. The owner asked if we could pay the tax and license fees that day. I asked him how much. When his response was $206.50, Cheryl and I smiled as we paid $3.50 along with the gift offering from the church (mentioned above). A couple of months later the balance owed on the car was given to us as a gift.

I have often reflected on this story and how it relates to our personal relationship with God, and how God wants us to put that relationship with Him above everything. He really does want us to trust Him in all things pertaining to life and godliness. That's what being a Christian is all about.

"Consequently, you are no longer foreigners and aliens, but fellow citizens with God's people and members of God's household, built on the foundation of the apostles and prophets, with Christ Jesus himself as the chief cornerstone. In him the whole building is

joined together and rises to become a holy temple in the Lord. And in him you too are being built together to become a dwelling in which God lives by his Spirit" (Ephesians 2:19-22). NIV

"As you come to him, the living Stone—rejected by men but chosen by God and precious to him—you also, like living stones, are being built into a spiritual house to be a holy priesthood, offering spiritual sacrifices acceptable to God through Jesus Christ. For in Scripture it says: 'See, I lay a stone in Zion, a chosen and precious cornerstone, and the one who trusts in him will never be put to shame.' Now to you who believe, this stone is precious. But to those who do not believe, 'The stone the builders rejected has become the capstone,' and, 'A stone that causes men to stumble and a rock that makes them fall.' They stumble because they disobey the message—which is also what they were destined for. But you are a chosen people, a royal priesthood, a holy nation, a people belonging to God, that you may declare the praises of him who called you out of darkness into his wonderful light" (1Peter 2:4-9). NIV

This is what the journey is all about, a kingdom of priests, a holy nation, and the people of God being built up together in the Holy Spirit. Living in the kingdom now is about our relationship with Him as the Cornerstone, and then about our relationship with each other as His priests. Brotherly love is the hallmark of the true and faithful Christian.

The call to freedom in Christ is not a call for greater individual independence. Rather it is a call to greater dependence on Christ. Freedom is a thing to be grasped only through total surrender to the keeper of our soul. Freedom is not rebellion but contrition that leads to restoration. Christ restores the inner man giving him freedom that sets him free.

Remember that bedrock is the solid rock beneath the soil and superficial rock. It is a secure foundation on which rivers run. It is the very bottom. The term bedrock is also described as basic principles and facts. As we view the term in this book, let us visualize it as the place on which the kingdom of God flows.

Our journey will take us many places, but let us keep in mind this visual picture. Bedrock is not a place, a denomination, a particular church, or movement. Bedrock is the visionary place where Christian people everywhere see the Church without walls and divisions. They are the Christians who, with courage, walk by the Spirit and listen to the Father's heart.

"Let us hold fast the confession of our hope without wavering, for He who promised is faithful; and let us consider how to stimulate one another to love and good deeds, not forsaking our own assembling together, as is the habit of some, but encouraging one another; and all the more, as you see the day drawing near" (Hebrews 10:23-25).

Pray that God will give you a dream, a vision, a work to do. Finding bedrock is about the joy of achieving God's purpose and plan for your life. It's about stirring up and using the spiritual gifts inside you. It's about going for the gold with God on your side. Remember, the gifts and callings of God are irrevocable.

"It was for freedom that Christ set us free; therefore keep standing firm and do not be subject again to a yoke of slavery" (Galatians 5:1).

There's a crack in the Christian liberty bell of freedom, and instead of the "Clarion Call" to unity in the body of Christ being loud and shrill, it is dull and soft. Rise up, O Church of God! Rise up and sound the alarm! God is forging a new "Liberty Bell," not out of dross, but forged out of pure gold in those with pure hearts. The "Clarion Call" for unity is like myriads and myriads of holy angels singing to God in the highest: *"Hallelujah! Salvation and glory belong to our God. Hallelujah! For the Lord our God, the Almighty, reigns. Let us rejoice and be glad and give the glory to Him, for the marriage of the Lamb has come and the bride has made herself ready" (Revelation selected).*

2

Riding the White Horse – Truth!

"The works of His hands are truth and justice; all His precepts are sure" (Psalm 111:7).

Martin Luther was opposed to Roman Catholic authority, to salvation by works, and he believed that the church held people captive to and through the sacraments. I believe people are held captive the same way today, but through division, sectarianism, and denominationalism. Jesus said, *"For where two or three have gathered together in My name, there I am in their midst" (Matthew 18:20).*

Truth equals freedom. *"I am the way, and the truth, and the life; no one comes to the Father, but through Me" (John 14:6).* JESUS!

"If you abide in My word, then you are truly disciples of mine; and you shall know the truth, and the truth shall make you free" (John 8:31,32). JESUS!

The quest for truth is never more evident than when one is in trouble. When in trouble, people often open their hearts to God; that is, if their pride isn't in the way. For many years I ministered in jails, prisons, and rescue missions. During these years I saw many desperate men looking for answers and finding those answers in a personal relationship with Jesus. The best time to search for answers, though, is before your situation becomes desperate. As long as your life is rolling along without major incidence or problems, you are the one who feels in control. This concept is the ultimate in delusion and one of Satan's most effective weapons. Let us now attempt to cut delusion to shreds in order to find the heart of truth.

"Truly, truly, I say unto you, unless one is born again, he cannot see the kingdom of God" (John 3:3). JESUS!

"Truly, truly," is the starting point of what Jesus had to say about eternal life and living in the kingdom of God. It is not about whether or not you want to be born again. Salvation is God's requirement for entering the kingdom of God. Jesus came as God in the flesh, and being God, He was incapable of lying. Therefore, truth is the base of everything He had to say. If we cannot accept what Jesus said as truth, we are calling

Him a liar, and if He is a liar, we must reject it all. One thing we cannot do, though, is to remain neutral.

Truth should be the abiding place of the human soul, for without it, we are incapable of entering into personal relationship with God. When He brings forth truth, we must interact in kind.

Twenty-five times in John's Gospel, Jesus begins His exhortation with the words, "Truly, truly," or "Amen, amen," or "So be it, so be it." This is an important point because it was Christ who created the earth and it was Him who spoke it into existence.

"God, after He spoke long ago to the fathers in the prophets in many portions and in many ways, in these last days has spoken through His Son, whom He appointed heir of all things, through whom He also made the world. And He is the radiance of His glory and the exact representation of His nature, and upholds all things by the word of His power. When He had made purification of sins, He sat down at the right hand of the Majesty on high" (Hebrews 1:1-3).

It is what it is, because God spoke it. In the Gospel of John, "amen" is used at the beginning of sentences rather than the end. It is the announcing of truth at the inception. Truth and freedom are inseparable and dependent on each other. Freedom can be obtained no other way, particularly in spiritual matters. To the believer in Christ, He is our total reality and reality is truth. Truth must be the one thing that sets the Christian apart from the world, because it is the mark of the true and faithful Christian. In the same way, the archenemy of truth is Satan. He is a liar and the father of lies. If in any way he can deceive us, he will.

Jesus' declarations of truth are about heaven, eternal life, and about who can enter and who cannot. It is about living life without judgment and about eternal works that will last. It is about eating the bread of life and being satisfied. It is most about following One Shepherd and living in communion with Him. Living in the kingdom of God is also about being set free from sin.

Truth is not relative. It does not adjust to circumstance or to human will and desire. People cannot create their own truth. Truth stands on its own. God looks into your heart and knows all the truth about you.

Jesus said, *"There is nothing covered that will not be revealed, and hidden that will not be known. What I tell you in the darkness, speak in the light; and what you hear whispered in your ear, proclaim upon the housetops"* (Matthew 10:26,27).

Today, like no generation before, we are inundated with all kinds of deception. Deception attempts to suppress the truth.

"For the wrath of God is revealed from heaven against all ungodliness and unrighteousness of men who suppress the truth in unrighteousness, *because that which is known about God is evident within them; for God made it evident to them" (Romans 1: 18,19).*

A well-known network news anchorman recently said, "Truth is never absolute, but more often compromise." And then he winked at us as he told us (in effect) that he was compromising what he declared as truth. Yet night after night, people will tune him back in, and at the same time they will tune God out.

Another example of relative truth is known as the "Liar's Loophole," which states: "My purposes are so noble, and the purposes of my enemies are so bad, that whatever I do to advance my purposes is justified." Relative truth says there is no (one) right way; whatever is truth to you is your truth. Relativism is morally unthinkable. It would excuse all immoral behavior such as: ethnic cleansing, slavery, abortion, euthanasia, prostitution, or even creation of a belief system based on deception, fantasy, and myths.

Listed below are some examples of common forms that can be used to deceive and divide:

Fantasy – imagination
Myth – fictitious story
Legend – non-verifiable story
Custom – a habit inspired by tradition
Illusion – mocking deceit
Tradition – surrender or betrayal to stories, beliefs, and customs
Delusion – false belief that is contrary to fact or reality

In Christianity, truth is always absolute and must never be compromised. Jesus did not come to earth to defy our reason and intellect, but to define it. This is the ultimate reality of truth: *"I am the way, and the truth, and the life; no one comes to the Father, but through Me"* (John 14:6).

Any philosophy, person, or religious group that seeks to make Jesus mysterious and abstract, rather than personal, opens the door to the spirit of deception and the spirit of man-made religion.

The revelation of Jesus Christ is the revelation of God. Truth does pass the test of revelation and prophesy. There are around 730 prophecies concerning the coming Messiah recorded in the Holy Scriptures, and Jesus fulfilled them all. Had He failed to fulfill just one of them, He would not be the true Messiah. Jesus is not a myth, or legend, or a tradition, or fantasy, or custom, or illusion, or delusion. He is God. Jesus came in the flesh, died for our sins on the cross, and rose from the dead. He was then, and is now, the reality of the ages. He is the Christ.

As we consider the truth of the gospel, we should also remember that unity among the community of believers is about laboring in His vineyard. I think that my upcoming simple story, Down on the Farm, illustrates the present condition of the vineyard. I have used the term farm rather than vineyard because it makes for easier story telling.

Down on the Farm

One day I went to visit a farm and I liked what the farmer had to say about farming. So for the next five years I went to learn as much from this farmer as I could, because he was a very good farmer. My circumstances did not allow me to stay and I had to move away.

Still interested in farming, I began to visit other farms. Some of these farms were good and others lacked the right soil, or the right fertilizer, or the right seed. In some places the soil was too rocky, and in others there were too many thorny berry bushes growing in the field. Every time you got too close to one you would get pricked with thorns. Some of the thorn bushes were already dead and it was hard to see the thorns and those were the ones that hurt the most.

Some of these farms had the best farming equipment you could get. But many farmers had a hard time finding people to operate the equipment. One place I went to had just built a new barn, but had no one who knew anything about farming.

An explorer showed up one day to share what he knew about exploring and ended up as the farmer. He became a very good and successful farmer. All the farm hands loved him and worked hard for him, maybe because he had the heart of an explorer. I also worked on this farm for awhile and learned from this farmer. I got more and more excited about farming and somehow knew I was supposed to become a farmer, too.

So, I went off to farming school to learn more. I learned a little, but decided I did not want to be a farmer after all. I still loved hanging around the farm. After awhile farming got so much into my blood that I just had to learn more, so I went to farming school again. I never wanted to own a farm, I just wanted to tell everyone about farming and about how great it was to live on the farm.

I left farming school for a short time to work on a very special kind of farm. At this farm they helped a lot of people who felt out of place on the regular farms. It was great work experience but I just felt I needed to learn more about farming so I could become the best possible helper to the farmer.

This time, at farming school, I learned that I was an unusual kind of farmer. I had a vision of seeing all the farmers working together. I saw one big field where all the farms were working with one purpose to produce the best and the biggest possible crop. I thought perhaps they could share with each other their farming equipment, knowledge, and experience. Maybe, in this way, all of the things that were dividing the farms (such as rocks and trees and brush and thistles) could be eliminated. To my amazement, though, I found out that the farmers did not want this, nor did they appreciate my efforts to join these farms together. What they wanted me to do was to start my own farm and not mess with their fences.

Then I found out that one man owned all the farms, so I made an appointment with him to find out what he thought about my plan. He told me that it was his plan all along and that he didn't like the fences either. He told me that I needed to continue in my efforts to take down the fences because he had good pastureland just beyond the fences, for those farmers who would be willing to give him the fences. Truth be known, we are all just farmers.

Yes, we really are all just farmers working in His vineyard. Perhaps this simplistic story has given you a vision beyond the fences.

"And I saw heaven standing open and there before me was a white horse, whose rider is called Faithful and True. With justice he judges and makes war. His eyes are like blazing fire, and on his head are many crowns. He has a name written on him that no one knows but he himself. He is dressed in a robe dipped in blood, and his name is the Word of God. The armies of heaven were following him, riding on white horses and dressed in fine linen, white and clean. Out of his mouth comes a sharp sword with which to strike down the nations. 'He will rule them with an iron scepter.' He treads the winepress of the fury of the wrath of God Almighty. On his robe and on his thigh he has this name written: KING OF KINGS AND LORD OF LORDS" (Revelation 19:11-16). NIV

It is hard to believe, I know, but there are no fences in heaven.

3

The History Lesson

"There is an appointed time for everything. And there is a time for every event under heaven. He has made everything appropriate in its time" (Ecclesiastes 3:1,11).

Throughout the history of the Church, there were a few major events that altered humanity's course and direction. As we begin this journey to find the bedrock on which the river of God flows, it is important to remember that God is holy, the Bible is a holy book, and that heaven is a holy place. Christ's Church on the other hand is not holy or perfect. There will always be weeds among the wheat. To see the Church as holy is often where the greatest misunderstandings and misconceptions about God begin. Even as we individually consider ourselves as members of Christ's Church here on earth, we struggle with our own unrighteousness, knowing we are not holy. Then we remember that we are made righteous through Christ's blood. And because we are, we struggle out of a sense of gratitude to meet Christ's expectations. Our own conflict comes when the institutional church fails to meet our expectations. Yes, it seems that we are people with great contradictions.

This book is intended to flesh out some of the perplexities found in the Christian religion. We must overcome the temptation to rely on reason alone, for the journey with God is mostly a walk of faith through the Spirit. God is a God who justifies men by faith and not by reason and intellect.

"For consider your calling, brethren, that there were not many wise according to the flesh, not many mighty, not many noble; but God has chosen the foolish things of the world to shame the wise, and God has chosen the weak things of the world to shame the things which are strong, and the base things of the world and the despised, God has chosen, the things that are not, that He might nullify the things that are, that no man should boast before God. But by His doing you are in Christ Jesus, who became to us wisdom from God, and righteousness and sanctification, and redemption, that, just as it is written, 'Let him who boasts, boast in the Lord'" (1 Corinthians 1:26-31).

It is generally assumed that recorded history is an accurate chronicle of time and events. In reality, history is more accurately a mix of facts, legends, tales, romance, and subjective information recorded by those who see history through their window. It has been said that the winners, not the losers, write history.

One day my wife, Cheryl, was seeking the Lord at the creek that runs by our house. Her question to the Lord was, "What is in the way of a major spiritual revival?" The Lord spoke to her, "Legends of man."

Legends of man means: an unverified popular tale handed down from earlier times. Many people hold on to family legends as though they were right and true—kind of like a sacred trust. Yet rarely do they understand the foundation and intricacies of these beliefs and tales. Many of the legends are so ingrained in the spiritual life of a person that they interfere with objective analysis of truth. Many, without questioning the validity of these legends, accept and adopt them into their belief system as truth. Truth cannot be subjective, only objective.

Legends of man can also be the looking to the local folk, sport, political, and religious heroes for life's solutions and fulfillment. Images of these people have an influence on us and often shape the direction of our lives. In today's world, visual and verbal deception and fantasy are our major forms of entertainment. Almost everything seen on television for example is an illusion or deception – not real. Young people live with dreams of being like Michael Jordan, Bill Gates, or some other person they idolize. Belief systems based on tolerance and relativism become ideals for ethical and moral decision-making in our current culture. Tolerance leads to apathy. Apathy leads to flight.

People tend to follow people. People should follow God. Jesus said, *"Seek first the kingdom and His righteousness" (Matthew 6:33).*

The Lord Yahweh is the author of all history. He is not a legend or a tale. He is the burning reality of truth, life, light, and eternity. His message to us is that He writes the book of life and records the names found there. The Lamb's book of life is the only book one needs to be concerned about.

In Revelation 21:27 NIV, while talking about heaven the text states, *"Nothing impure will ever enter it, nor will anyone who does what is shameful or deceitful, but only those whose names are written in the Lamb's book of life."*

Whatever men say about you does not matter. If your name is not found in His book, all your good works and achievements on earth won't count anyway. *"And I saw the dead, great and small, standing before the throne, and books were opened. Another book was opened, which is the book of life. The dead were judged according to what they had done as recorded in the books. The sea gave up the dead that were in it, and death and Hades gave up the dead that were in them, and each person was judged according to what he had done. Then death and Hades were thrown into the lake of fire. The lake of fire is the second death. If anyone's name was not found written in the book of life, he was thrown into the lake of fire" (Revelation 20:12-15). NIV*

"Someone in the crowd said to him, 'Teacher, tell my brother to divide the inheritance with me.' Jesus

replied, 'Man, who appointed me a judge or an arbiter between you?' Then he said to them, 'Watch out! Be on your guard against all kinds of greed; a man's life does not consist in the abundance of his possessions.' And he told them this parable: 'The ground of a certain rich man produced a good crop. He thought to himself, "What shall I do? I have no place to store my crops." Then he said, "This is what I'll do. I will tear down my barns and build bigger ones, and there I will store all my grain and my goods. And I'll say to myself, 'You have plenty of good things laid up for many years. Take life easy; eat, drink and be merry.'" But God said to him, 'You fool! This very night your life will be demanded from you. Then who will get what you have prepared for yourself?' 'This is how it will be with anyone who stores up things for himself but is not rich toward God.' Then Jesus said to his disciples: 'Therefore I tell you, do not worry about your life, what you will eat; or about your body, what you will wear. Life is more than food, and the body more than clothes. Consider the ravens: They do not sow or reap, they have no storeroom or barn; yet God feeds them. And how much more valuable you are than birds! Who of you by worrying can add a single hour to his life? Since you cannot do this very little thing, why do you worry about the rest? Consider how the lilies grow. They do not labor or spin. Yet I tell you, not even Solomon in all his splendor was dressed like one of these. If that is how God clothes the grass of the field, which is here today, and tomorrow is thrown into the fire, how much more will he clothe you, O you of little faith! And do not set your heart on what you will eat or drink; do not worry about it. For the pagan world runs after all such things, and your Father knows that you need them. But seek his kingdom, and these things will be given to you as well. Do not be afraid, little flock, for your Father has been pleased to give you the kingdom. Sell your possessions and give to the poor. Provide purses for yourselves that will not wear out, a treasure in heaven that will not be exhausted, where no thief comes near and no moth destroys. For where your treasure is, there your heart will be also'" (Luke 12:13-34). NIV

Much of what we believe about God and religion is culturally derived. Cultural influence has a lot to do with one's perception of the institutional church. We are impacted by the broadness and complexities of culture that includes: the media, nationalism, and the history lessons that our particular government and society deems important. Additionally, our beliefs are also shaped by the immediate culture of our families, religious training, and peers.

History can become the laboratory for the future. Time belongs to God and He is infinite. We can usher nothing in unless He is the Usher. We can, however, look into the past to see in part where we have come from; yet we are limited by time and culture. So we look at the past with caution, and at the things of God with confidence through His revealed Word. Breathe on us now Holy Spirit.

The History Lesson

The religious heritage that believers have should be highly esteemed by all Christians. The Church fathers and martyrs have given us a rich inheritance. Our Christian brothers and sisters, past and present, have and are diligently preserving the accuracy and integrity of the Word of God. We all owe them our deepest gratitude. Integrity is not always achieved through popular approval, but the test of time.

The early Church fathers protected us from heresy and helped to define orthodox Christian theology. Anyone who has given his or her life to the ministry of the Gospel should always be appreciated. Many of God's great saints have given their lives translating the Bible into different languages and dialects. Missionaries have taken the Bible message to remote places around the globe. The Bible has inspired writers and poets and musicians and artists and scientists and adventurers and scholars and teachers and politicians and mothers and fathers and human rights activists and soldiers on the battlefield and children. Christians throughout the past twenty centuries have given their lives as laborers and martyrs to evangelize the world for Christ. Those who are believers in Christ today should examine their willingness to do the same.

Now let us explore the various ways history, culture, time, and events have influenced and shaped our religious thinking. Many people mistakenly believe that the Jewish synagogue in Jesus' time was much like the traditional church today. In order to best understand how the church structure came to be, we should first look at Jewish culture and their religious system at the time of Christ.

To the Jew—religious, cultural, and political life, were all a part of the same thing. The meeting places leading up to the time of Christ were synagogues. The synagogue was not mentioned in the Old Testament. The synagogue became necessary during their Babylonian captivity and became the meeting place for Jews during the Roman occupation. There were 394 synagogues in Jerusalem in A.D. 70.

The purpose of the synagogue was for worship, social life, education, cultural life, and government. They were nothing like the traditional church we know today. Synagogues promoted Jewish nationalism and Jewish solidarity. The same scenario is true today. Synagogues are ethnic centers that support Jewish causes. Synagogues became a convenient meeting place for early Christians. They also served as a starting place for Christian missionaries. When Titus destroyed Jerusalem in A.D. 70, Jewish nationalism in Israel ended. Then in 1948, the new State of Israel was chartered by the United Nations.

When Christ rebuked the scribes and the Pharisees, He was attacking the leadership of Israel, political and religious. In the Old Testament, these leaders were often referred to as the shepherds of Israel. This term shepherd was a common metaphor in the ancient Near East for ruler. Lawyers also fell into this camp.

Christ had great compassion on the masses of people who were being neglected by the leaders of His day. Jesus did not come for the purpose of adding credence and endorsement to the Jewish religion, but to offer salvation to all mankind. Jesus was not trying to reform Judaism, but to fulfill all the promises and covenants He made to them. Jesus came to set the captives free! Those who Jesus has set free are free indeed.

There have been many significant events that have shaped church history. The early Church was greatly influenced philosophically, governmentally, and culturally by Greek and Roman thought. Many of the early heresies in Christianity came from these schools of thought. As we attempt to look through the layers of history in order to rediscover the foundations of Christianity, let us remain objective in our pursuit of early bedrock Christianity. Historians often attempt to give both excuses and justification for the failures of society.

Several notable historical events have impacted church development. In A.D. 313, the Edict of Milan, issued by Constantine the Great, guaranteed freedom and tolerance of all religions in the Roman Empire. The First Council of Nicea established Jesus as the "true God of true God" in A.D. 325. The Council of Chalcedon in A.D. 451 wrote the Nicene Creed. The creed resolved the two natures of Christ. This creed affirmed Jesus' full humanity and full divinity. In other words, the creed cements to fact that Jesus is fully God and He is (at the same time) fully man. Another notable historical event occurred in 1456, when Johann Gutenberg produced the first printed book, the Bible. In 1611, the authorized King James Bible was published in English.

Controversy and factions have plagued and divided the Church for the past fifteen hundred years. The first major division came in A.D. 1054, and is known as the Great Schism between Eastern and Western Christianity. This event still divides Eastern Orthodox Christians and Roman Catholics. Then, in 1095, Pope Urban II launched the first crusade to drive Moslems from the Holy Land. In 1378, there was "The Great Papal Schism" in which two popes, and later three, vied for supremacy in the medieval church. The crisis lasted for forty years.

No doubt, the greatest controversy that reshaped the Church began in 1517, when Martin Luther posted the Ninety-Five Theses on the door of the church in Wittenberg, Germany. That act of defiance by Luther started the Protestant Reformation. This event, coupled with putting the Bible into the hands of ordinary people, changed the complexion of the Church until this very day.

There are still other notable events that have further widened the gap between Christians that should also be mentioned. "The Wars of Religion" in France, carried out by ultra-orthodox Catholics against Protestants, resulted in the massacre of thousands. On September 8, 1572, Rome celebrated these despicable acts of carnage with a "Mass of Thanks" for the great grace received of God.

Anglican and Episcopal denominations were established when the British Parliament elected King Henry VIII as the head of the Church of England.

And John Calvin's 1536 work ("Institutes of the Christian Religion") shaped the Presbyterian and Reformed denominations.

In 1545, at the "Council of Trent," the Catholic Church started its own reformation that condemned Protestant views and set the course for Catholicism to this day.

Many other movements and denominations have attempted to redefine and clarify Christianity. In 1738, John Wesley began a preaching ministry that birthed the Methodist movement. There were also the Puritans, Moravians, and Quakers who birthed sects of their own. Perhaps one of the most significant events in recent times occurred in Los Angles at the 1906 Azusa Street Revival. The outpouring of the Holy Spirit at this revival gave birth to many new Pentecostal denominations.

At times, history has also led us into darkness, theological elitism, spiritual instability, liberalism, and spiritual abuse. Unfortunately, this dark side of Christianity is also a part of our history. It has caused a knee-jerk reaction of justified skepticism regarding the validity of some ministries. The enemy has used these attitudes of suspicion to prevent many from embracing the true gospel. If you are able, try to set these things of history aside. Christianity is more about freedom than failure. When we look at others we tend walk in judgment. But when we keep our eyes on Christ, we can walk in freedom.

When we look at Christian history, we must look at what God has done with much greater weight than what man has done. Because, where man has messed it up, God has straightened it out. God is God. We are His process.

4

Double Vision

"And it will come about after this that I will pour out My Spirit on all mankind; and your sons and daughters will prophesy, your old men will dream dreams, your young men will see visions" (Joel 2:28).

I believe that God speaks to man primarily through His Word, the Bible. I also believe He speaks to us in prayer, visions, dreams, in our thoughts, and occasionally through others, and always through the Helper, the Holy Spirit. Yes! God also speaks to us through nature. All of these avenues used by God come as revelations to us in order to encourage us in our personal walk with Him. We grow in God from revelation to revelation.

Testing the spirits

"Dear friends, do not believe every spirit, but test the spirits to see whether they are from God, because

many false prophets have gone out into the world. This is how you can recognize the Spirit of God: Every spirit that acknowledges that Jesus Christ has come in the flesh is from God, but every spirit that does not acknowledge Jesus is not from God. This is the spirit of the antichrist, which you have heard is coming and even now is already in the world. You, dear children, are from God and have overcome them, because the one who is in you is greater than the one who is in the world. They are from the world and therefore speak from the viewpoint of the world, and the world listens to them. We are from God, and whoever knows God listens to us; but whoever is not from God does not listen to us. This is how we recognize the Spirit of truth and the spirit of falsehood" (1 John 4:1-6). NIV

When the early believers in Christ got together for fellowship, they shared the truth about God and the revelations God was giving them. Christians still seek the leading of the Holy Spirit for guidance, direction, and help. Spiritual sensitivity and prayer help us to determine what is from God and what is not from God. If the revelation lines up with the Bible, and is in accord with God's plan for your life, it is probably from God. If it is overly mystical and weird—pray through—seek wise spiritual counsel, or wait until God gives you the interpretation or confirmation.

Sometimes dreams and visions take the form of illustrations that teach us deeper spiritual truths. In this book you will read some of these dreams, visions, story illustrations, and revelations that bring insight and emphasis to the direction of the book.

The "body of Christ" should judge dreams, visions, and prophetic utterances that are spoken in congregant church settings. Although we no longer stone the false prophet—we still should bring false prophesies into judgment. Throughout the Old Testament, God spoke to His prophets in visions and dreams. We often think of the dreams of Joseph and Daniel. The Lord also spoke through many, many others in dreams and visions as well. Jesus was the fulfillment of all the Messianic prophesies. But there are still many prophesies, in both the Old and New Testaments concerning the second coming of Jesus, yet to be fulfilled.

Most of us would like to know what is coming next. If we could see for certain, even one day into the future, that would be unique. But sorcery and witchcraft is not an option for the Christian. However, the Bible gives us glimpses into the future when we are diligent to study the prophecies.

In this age, many of the end-time prophecies are being fulfilled; yet, there are still many we do not understand. I believe we are living in the last days. The Bible has given us ample warning concerning what we need to do to get prepared for the final days.

Unfortunately many people are not listening. And then the end will come without warning—bang, it's over. Jesus said, *"Behold, I am coming like a thief. Blessed is the one who stays awake and keeps his garments, lest he walk about naked and men see his shame" (Revelation 16:15).*

The good news is that Christ is raising up a remnant people who are sold out to God and are getting ready for His second coming. They are the ones who have not soiled their garments or been polluted by the things of the world. They are the ones who will walk with Jesus, dressed in white, for they will be considered worthy. There are also some people who live in the camp of the lukewarm and the comfortable who are in danger of not obtaining the prize—eternal life. Some think they have received just enough from God to go to heaven. Perhaps they need to find the gold found in the relationship with the Father, and anoint their eyes so they can see the obvious.

"Come now, let us reason together, says the Lord, though your sins be as scarlet, they will be white as snow; though they be red like crimson, they will be like wool" (Isaiah 1:18).

When you accept Jesus into your heart, He blots out your sins with His own blood and sees them no more. It's like He has handed you a clean piece of white paper, with nothing written on it, and said to you: "This is the record of your sins." Then He fills you with the Holy Spirit and begins to give you new dreams and visions for the future.

Dreams and visions of spirit-filled Christians should not be considered weird or unusual or mystical. Believers filled with the Holy Spirit should be seeking the will of God in their lives. It is appropriate to seek dreams and visions because they are a part of the believer's own individual Pentecost. *"And your young men shall see visions and your old men shall dream dreams" (Acts 2:17c).*

All who have accepted Jesus into their hearts have been given spiritual gifts, but not all are using them. Some are not aware of the gifts. Others don't use the gifts because of unbelief. And there are others who are fearful of the gifts. Those who believe in the spiritual gifts—use them. Those who do not believe are missing out on all that God has for them. The spiritual gifts are for today, *"For the promise is for you and your children, and for all who are far off, as many as the Lord shall call to Himself" (Acts 2:39).*

Double Vision

Spiritual dreams and visions may come as a result of seeking God for direction, through prayer with a sincere heart. If you don't want His direction in your life, don't pray. When God gives you direction, pray for confirmation. God oftentimes gives people a "double vision." Here are a couple of examples:

"In Damascus there was a disciple named Ananias. The Lord called to him in a vision, 'Ananias!' 'Yes, Lord,' he answered. The Lord told him, 'Go to the house of Judas on Straight Street and ask for a man from Tarsus named Saul, for he is praying. In a vision he has seen a man named Ananias come and place his hands on him to restore his sight'" (Acts 9:10-12). NIV

Notice the detail and how Ananias and Paul both shared the same vision. The next example is found in the tenth chapter of Acts.

"While Peter was wondering about the meaning of the vision, the men sent by Cornelius found out where Simon's house was and stopped at the gate. They called out, asking if Simon who was known as Peter was staying there. While Peter was still thinking about the vision, the Spirit said to him, 'Simon, three men are looking for you. So get up and go downstairs. Do not hesitate to go with them, for I have sent them.' Peter went down and said to the men, 'I'm the one you're looking for. Why have you come?' The men replied, 'We have come from Cornelius the centurion. He is a righteous and God-fearing man, who is respected by all the Jewish people. A holy angel told him to have you come to his house so that he could hear what you have to say'" (Acts 10:17-22). NIV

Spiritual dreams and visions require spiritual sensitivity and obedience to the vision. If you will not be compliant to the leading of the Holy Spirit in these things, why would you expect God to give you dreams and visions? God expects you to take action on what He shows you. If we are following God's plan, He will put the unknown parts together; after all, it's His plan. God's best plan for us is always better than our imagination. Our vain imaginations often lead us away from the spiritual realities of kingdom living. We can easily be seduced by worldly ambitions.

Double Vision

Here's then another vision example:

"Paul and his companions traveled throughout the region of Phrygia and Galatia, having been kept by the Holy Spirit from preaching the word in the province of Asia. When they came to the border of Mysia, they tried to enter Bithynia, but the Spirit of Jesus would not allow them to. So they passed by Mysia and went down to Troas. During the night Paul had a vision of a man of Macedonia standing and begging him, 'Come over to Macedonia and help us.' After Paul had seen the vision, we got ready at once to leave for Macedonia, concluding that God had called us to preach the gospel to them. From Troas we put out to sea and sailed straight for Samothrace, and the next day on to Neapolis. From there we traveled to Philippi, a Roman colony and the leading city of that district of Macedonia. And we stayed there several days. On the Sabbath we went outside the city gate to the river, where we expected to find a place of prayer. We sat down and began to speak to the women who had gathered there. One of those listening was a woman named Lydia, a dealer in purple cloth from the city of Thyatira, who was a worshiper of God. The Lord opened her heart to respond to Paul's message. When she and the members of her household were baptized, she invited us to her home. 'If you consider me a believer in the Lord,' she said, 'come and stay at my house.' And she persuaded us" (Acts 16:6-15). NIV

Spiritual people with a vision and a dream should not become discouraged, but hang onto their dreams.

When I was in Bible College, I became friends with a man named Harvey Frank. Harvey was one of God's great miracles of redemption. He had been in prison, and was a heroin addict and a thief. He was saved and miraculously delivered from heroin addiction through the Teen Challenge program in Brooklyn, New York. He became a counselor for them and then graduated from Central Bible College, Springfield, Missouri, in 1989. We stayed in touch after he graduated.

God gave Harvey the passion and the dream of going to Eastern Europe to minister the gospel. He and his family ministered with Christ for the Nations. Living in a bus, they traveled all over Eastern Europe, preaching the good news of Jesus Christ with great success. God gave Harvey the desire of his heart. After returning to the States, he and his family established a home base in Nebraska.

Not long after their return home, I received a call from Harvey telling me the worst. He had brain cancer and the prognosis wasn't good. He started chemotherapy immediately. We decided at that time to meet somewhere between Nebraska and Arizona (where I was then living), for fellowship and prayer. We both felt that was what God wanted.

We arranged to meet in Colorado Springs, Colorado. He was going to drive from Beaverton, Nebraska, and pick me up at the airport in Colorado Springs. My flight arrived on time at 12:00 p.m., but Harvey was nowhere to be found. I called his home and there was no answer. I waited around till after 1:00 p.m., then decided to rent a car and go visit friends. I drove north for about one hour before I realized I had lost a carry-on bag with my camera and other valuables in it. Furious with myself, I turned the car around and headed back to Colorado Springs. I questioned God with "Why do these things happen?"

I returned to the rental car booth where I recovered my bag. Praise God! It was now about 4:00 p.m., and I headed upstairs to mail some letters I had carried along. I then went back downstairs to where the phones were, to try to call Harvey's home. As I approached the phones, guess who was standing there? That's right; it was Harvey. He had just arrived, over four hours late. But God's timing was perfect. Now I knew why I had lost the carry-on bag!

Harvey had left Nebraska for Colorado Springs at 5:00 p.m. the previous day. He wanted to give himself plenty of time in case he had car trouble. While going through Kansas, he experienced double vision and was driving on the wrong side of the road. Fortunately, a policeman pulled him over. Thinking he was drunk, the officer arrested Harvey and took him to the police station. Harvey finally convinced the officer that his driving problem was a result of his illness.

Harvey's wife, Kathy, came with a friend and drove him back home. Harvey went immediately to bed, and awoke at midnight. He told his wife he needed to go to Colorado to meet me. Kathy pleaded with him to stay home, but Harvey was determined. He drove all night and stopped in the early morning for a little rest. He arrived in Colorado Springs late but without problem or incidence.

When I saw Harvey, and when he saw me, we knew God had performed a miracle. We spent the next couple of days together discussing the future. We stayed in a nice hotel, ate a great dinner together, went to see *Focus on the Family* headquarters, and went sightseeing. It was good for Harvey, good for me, and blessed of the Lord.

Harvey returned home without experiencing any further problems on the trip. God was in it with us, and we dined with Him in His presence. Harvey fought a courageous battle with cancer, but went home to be with the Lord several months later. I was honored to go to Nebraska and officiate at his memorial service.

When God gives you a vision or a dream, stay with the dream. God is not like man who changes his mind. Don't become discouraged by circumstances and hardship. Be prepared to suffer shipwreck but not failure. God had told the Apostle Paul, in a vision, that he would proclaim the gospel message in Rome. Paul did suffer shipwreck on his way to Rome. All on the ship had given up hope of being saved (this includes Paul), but God was in control. It was His plan and not man's plan. *"The steps of a man are established by the Lord; and He delights in his way. When he falls, he shall not be hurled headlong; because the Lord is the one who holds his hand"* (Psalm 37:23,24).

Pray that God will give you a dream and a vision, and when He does:
1) Stay with the dream
2) Expect some problems
3) Defeat the enemy
4) And push through...
until you see and realize your dream.

Dreams, visions, and revelations are not so much about satisfying you as they are fulfilling God's purpose in your life. When your heart and will is bent toward God, God is in control of both your situation and your future.

Your Assignment

God has an assignment and purpose for you, a plan for your life. You are not here by random chance or cosmic accident. He is not a God of doom, sorrow, and despair. He is a God of hope, righteousness, peace, and joy. And within that righteousness, peace, and joy you will find your delight in Him. As you delight in Him, you will delight in your assignment. He will reveal truth to you through His Word, through dreams and visions, through prayer, through your righteous thoughts, and sometimes through the prophetic spoken word.

It is your own personal divine assignment. When He gives you your assignment, delight in it, for it is His best plan for you. Your best plan will lead to frustration, despair, and disappointment. His best plan will lead to light and life. God is not looking for you to become a religious professional. But He is looking for people who will reap the harvest and work in His vineyard.

Jesus said, *"The harvest is plentiful, but the workers are few. Therefore beseech the Lord of the harvest to send out workers into His harvest"* (Matthew 9: 37,38).

The delight in the Lord is found when you are a harvester picking grapes in His vineyard. You don't need to get permission to be a harvester, so pick away.

"Trust in the Lord and do good; dwell in the land and cultivate faithfulness. Delight yourself in the Lord; and He will give you the desires of your heart. Commit your way to the Lord, trust also in Him, and He will do it. And He will bring forth your righteousness as the light." (Psalm 37: 3-6).

5

Tensions of Revelation

"What I tell you in the darkness, speak in the light; and what you hear whispered in your ear, proclaim upon the housetops. Do not think that I came to bring peace on the earth; I did not come to bring peace, but a sword" (Matthew 10:27,34).

It was Saturday, January 2, 1999, when the Lord began to speak to me about attending a certain church in Eureka, on Sunday. At the time, it was a small independent church with about eleven adults and twenty-five children. I had only attended there one other time. On this Sunday, though, I was asked to share about the "Jericho March" our revival team was planning for the end of the month. I spoke for about fifteen minutes and returned to my seat.

On the way to church that morning, I had a conversation with my wife about going to the Netherlands in the year 2000, to preach revival. This was an idea the Lord had put into my mind and heart almost a year before. We agreed together in prayer that we would go if God provided the finances. God's response was almost immediate.

After the service, a man whom I had briefly met one time before, came up to me and said, "While I was worshipping the Lord this morning, God spoke to me and said that I need to give you something." Astonished, I asked him what. He said, "The Lord wants me to give you a 1956 Chevy." I was overjoyed and speechless. He was so excited I couldn't believe it. In fact, I think he was happier giving the car to me than I was receiving it. Yes, Jesus did say, "It is more blessed to give than to receive." I instantly saw it as God's provision for our trip to the Netherlands.

Something else also happened that day. I saw God as a caring Father who truly loved me. It was like He looked down from heaven and saw a hidden desire in my heart to again drive a 1956 Chevy. The man who gave me the car was 43 years old, the car was 43 years old, and I was born in 1943. Coincidence? I don't think so.

"Therefore once more I will astound these people with wonder upon wonder; the wisdom of the wise will perish, and the intelligence of the intelligent will vanish" (Isaiah 29:14). God sometimes astounds us with miracles too wonderful to explain.

Tensions of Revelation 51

As the Lord gives us revelation and direction, we must address the issues He brings before us. If we do not embrace the revelation, we miss the blessings He has bestowed upon us. Our vision is limited and we only see in part, so we walk according to the enlightenment He has given. Sometimes there is much tension that develops when God challenges us to move out of our comfort zones. As we consider these various revelations, try to move on the side of faith rather than common sense. God will ask you to do things that will defy your common sense. When your hearts and minds are open—you can be filled. When you are filled, you can pour out to others.

Whenever anyone discusses religion and supernatural things it usually brings along with it a great deal of opinion and passion. This book is filled with tension, passion, opinion, and truth. Therefore, receive the truth, consider the opinion, and fill your heart and mind with passion.

What is needed in the new millennium are lasting changes that bring real unity to the body of Christ, not merely cosmetic ones. The new revival or reformation or renewal or restoration or revolution must reestablish a code of purity and righteousness without rebellion toward God. Believers must be in compliance to the truth that offers men liberty and sets people free! I believe it is time to return to the ways and passion of the early Church. You cannot build the kingdom of

God on warm feelings alone. The kingdom must be built on obedience and submission to Christ.

In the quest to return to bedrock Christianity, we must dig deep, past the accumulation of religious tradition, ritual, mystery, superstition, opinion, and myth to discover the truth that applies to all men, everywhere, all the time. One of these essential biblical truths is unity among the community of believers in Christ. Unfortunately, this truth has been compromised in order to accommodate various and diverse sectarian views. It was during the Jericho March that the Lord revealed to me His will for His Church.

The first day of January 1999, the Lord put it into my mind to organize a Jericho March to pray for revival in the city of Eureka, California. We asked the people to walk or ride a certain route each day for a half-hour for the first six days, and on the seventh day to walk or ride for three and a half hours. At the conclusion of the march, we held a rally that lasted for almost seven hours. Many people participated in the rally.

During the course of the prayer walk, the Lord began to speak a word to me. Here is His word: "Religious walls that segregate Christians must come down; they divide the sheep and become the seedbed for spiritual pride. Denominationalism, sectarianism, Catholicism, and Christian cults are not biblical."

In the days and weeks that followed, I began to seek the Lord about this revelation, in conjunction with other revelations I had received in the Word. What I began to feel was a great deal of tension over the repercussions that would come as a result of preaching this message. So I decided to sit down and write about the feelings I was having—feelings I believe every Christian has when reading his or her Bible. Scriptures began to flood my mind. Here are some of them:

"Any kingdom divided against itself is laid waste; and a house divided against itself falls" (Luke 11:17).

"Then watch out that the light in you may not be darkness" (Luke 11:35).

"For nothing is hidden, except to be revealed; nor has anything been secret, but that it should come to light" (Mark 4:22).

"Strive to enter by the narrow door; for many, I tell you, will seek to enter, and will not be able" (Luke 13:24).

"For everyone who exalts himself shall be humbled, and he who humbles himself shall be exalted" (Luke 14:11).

"And He said to His disciples, 'It is inevitable that stumbling blocks should come, but woe to him through whom they come!'" (Luke 17:1).

"And do not judge and you will not be judged and do not condemn, and you will not be condemned; pardon, and you will be pardoned" (Luke 6:37).

Now is the time for Christians to deal with the tensions that exist within the Christian Church; that is to say, Roman Catholicism, and Protestantism. The main purpose for writing this book is the belief that the schisms that exist between the various groups within the Christian Church are actually inhibiting and stifling the growth of Christianity.

God is perfect—we are not. Therefore, the Church is not perfect. The revelation Jesus taught was that God is a jealous God. He desires man to be in relationship with Him so much that He was willing to send His Son Jesus to die for that purpose. Jesus died to set man free from sin, ritualistic legalism, religious tyranny, and the chains of death.

What Jesus died for set off a chain reaction revolution that turned the world 'right-side-up' for the next three centuries. The message that Christ Jesus had overcome death and the grave through resurrection, ignited hearts everywhere. Eternal salvation was now available to all men through acceptance of Jesus Christ as Lord and Savior, through the power of the Holy Spirit. Jesus preached that man could not obtain righteousness on his own.

The Apostle Paul put it this way, *"But that which is through faith in Christ, the righteousness which comes from God on the basis of faith, that I may know Him, and the power of His resurrection and the fellowship of His sufferings, being conformed to His death; in order that I may attain to the resurrection from the dead"* (Philippians 3:9-11).

In order for us to begin to resolve some of the tensions that exist in our hearts, we should find common agreement on the following topics. As we consider these six elements independently: restoration, liberty, responsibility, equality, unity, and stability, let us also consider how they relate to each other.

1) Restoration: And the Lord spoke to me saying, "I never wanted people to feel trapped by religion, but restored through relationship two ways; through Me and then through others." Restoration and reconciliation has always been God's plan. God loves you.

2) Liberty: *"It was for freedom that Christ set us free; therefore keep standing firm and do not be subject again to a yoke of slavery. For you were called to freedom, brethren; only do not turn your freedom into an opportunity for the flesh, but through love serve one another"* (Galatians 5:1,13). *"But one who looks intently at the perfect law, the law of liberty, and abides by it, not having become a forgetful hearer but an effectual doer, this man is blessed in what he does. So speak and so act, as those who are to be judged by the law of liberty. For judgment will be merciless to*

one who has shown no mercy; mercy triumphs over judgment" (James 1:25 & 2:12,13).

Christian liberty is extending, in full measure, the grace that was bestowed on you by the Father to your brothers and sisters in Christ.

3) Responsibility: Responsibility equals correct response and behavior. *"If you abide in My word, then you are truly disciples of Mine; and you shall know the truth, and the truth shall make you free" (John 8:31b, 32).* We must return to the truth that sets men free and leave the results of their freedom to God alone. We all know that freedom requires personal responsibility and that people need to become accountable for their freedom. As Peter said, *"Act as free men, and do not use your freedom as a covering for evil, but use it as bondslaves of God" (1 Peter 2:16).*

4) Equality: *"But you are a chosen people, a royal priesthood, a holy nation, a people belonging to God, that you may declare the praises of him who called you out of darkness into his wonderful light" (1 Peter 2:9). NIV* If we fail to emphasize the importance of the priesthood of all believers, we will fail to acknowledge the significant role each person plays as a priest before God.

5) Unity: *"And for their sakes I sanctify Myself, that they themselves may be sanctified in truth. I do*

not ask in behalf of these alone, but for those also who believe in Me through their word; that they may all be one; even as Thou, Father, art in Me, and I in Thee, that they also may be in Us; that the world may believe that Thou didst send Me. And the glory which Thou hast given Me I have given to them; that they may be one, just as We are one; I in them, and Thou in Me, that they may be perfected in unity, that the world may know that Thou didst send Me, and didst love them, even as Thou didst love Me" (John 17:19-23).

Why is unity in the church body so important? Jesus, in John 17, prays for Christians to be in oneness or unity four times. There are two reasons Jesus prayed this for us. Firstly, so the world may believe in God and His Son Jesus. Secondly, so the world may know that God sent His Son because He loved us so much. The unity prayer by Jesus is the most powerful statement in the Bible for evangelizing the world. We, as Christians, must overcome our differences in the body and embrace one another in Christ's love.

"Why do you judge your brother? Or you again, why do you regard your brother with contempt? For we shall all stand before the judgment seat of God" (Romans 14:10).

If salvation by grace is good enough for us personally, then it must also be good enough for our brother. Jesus said, *"A new commandment I give to you, that you love one another, even as I have loved you, that you also love one another. By this all men will know you are My disciples, if you have love for one another" (John 13:34,35).*

I have been troubled for sometime, as I know most Christians are, with the disunity we see in the body of Christ. I believe there is a direct correlation between the absence of unity and the absence of liberty that we should have in Christ. The other part of the equation is the issue of freedom, as promised in the Word of God to those who accept Christ by faith. I believe absence of one will reflect in the absence of the other, and vice versa. When we are in disunity, strife steals our liberty. When we feel restricted in our freedom to fellowship with others, we are in disunity. When we lose our freedom and unity, we are robbed of our peace and joy. It is all wrapped up in our relationship with God and our relationship with each other. When one is out of sync with the other, perpetual tension is the consequence.

In synchronized swimming, if just one swimmer is out of time with the others, the whole performance looks flawed. *"Beloved, let us love one another, for love is from God; and everyone who loves is born of God and knows God" (1 John 4:7).*

6) Stability: "Stability is not program, but righteousness, peace, and joy in the Holy Spirit."

I believe that resolving these six tensions between liberty and unity will bring restoration to the individual and the body of Christ.

As we continue our study on liberty and unity, various terms will arise. A good definition of those terms is necessary to avoid confusion and misunderstanding. Many of these terms have been used as a basis for division within the body of Christ. As we attempt to take down the religious walls that divide Christians, we should examine some of the terms that represent the walls in the first place.

Apostasy: The common classical use of the word is—a political defection. In the New Testament, its more usual meaning is a religious defection. Apostasy is secession from the faith and renouncing of Jesus. It is a departing from the faith, but not outward profession of it. Apostasy always relates to rebellion against God. (References: Acts 21:21; 1 Timothy 4:1; Hebrews 3:12; 2 Thessalonians 2:3; 2 Peter 3:17)

Heresy: Doctrinal departures from revealed truth, error. *"But avoid foolish controversies and genealogies and arguments and quarrels about the Law, because these are unprofitable and useless. Warn a divisive person once, and then warn him a second time. After that have nothing to do with him" (Titus 3:9,10).* NIV

"But there were also false prophets among the people, just as there will be false teachers among you. They will secretly introduce destructive heresies, even denying the sovereign Lord who bought them, bringing swift destruction on themselves" (2 Peter 2:1). NIV

Heresy disturbed the unity of doctrine and the unity of fellowship in the early church. The word heresy in the Greek means "sect" from which we get the word sectarian. Sectarian means to adhere to a dogmatic, narrow-minded, factional viewpoint.

Segregate: "To separate from the flock. To separate (a person, a body, or class of persons) from the general body, or some particular class, to set apart, isolate, seclude." Oxford Dictionary

Segregation: The action of segregating.

Schism: This word actually means division or separation. It is more accurately interpreted as one who has a tendency toward separation, one with a separatist heart.

Dogma: A system of doctrines proclaimed true by a religious sect. Dogma is a system of principles or belief.

Dogmatic: Marked by an authoritative, arrogant assertion of unproved principles.

Perhaps when we remove the religious walls that we have built in our own hearts and minds, real Christian unity will be a possibility. We must pray that God will reveal to each one individually what their religious walls are. Then we must pray that God will show us how to take the walls down. One's own personal prejudices and pride is where one can begin looking.

Jesus said, *"Do not judge, or you too will be judged. For in the same way you judge others, you will be judged, and with the measure you use, it will be measured to you. 'Why do you look at the speck of sawdust in your brother's eye and pay no attention to the plank in your own eye? How can you say to your brother, 'Let me take the speck out of your eye,' when all the time there is a plank in your own eye? You hypocrite, first take the plank out of your own eye, and then you will see clearly to remove the speck from your brother's eye"* (Matthew 7:1-5). NIV

6

Free at Last

"But take care lest this liberty of yours somehow become a stumbling block to the weak" (1 Corinthians 8:9).

This sermon message was first preached at a tent revival meeting we were having. The photo on the back cover was taken at this meeting. Notice too, the Lincoln Continental automobile that was mentioned in Chapter One.

I include this revival message because it is the basic polemic (or argument) for individual Christian liberty. The sermon is recorded here as it was preached to protect the accuracy of the revelation given to me by God.

During the writing of this sermon, my wife experienced one of the most violent cases of poison oak I have ever seen. Her experience, and the experience of others who went through this affliction, gave me some of the illustrations for this message.

Error or Heirs – Free at Last

This message has always been here in God's Word. This is not my word. It is God's word. I just did not understand the full impact and gospel intent of Christian liberty until now. I have always been troubled by those Scriptures which talk about freedom in Christ. Perhaps it is because I never experienced the full expression of the freedom that is promised in the Word. I pray that the Lord will speak into your lives the freedom Christ wants you to have.

Martin Luther was troubled by some of the same Scriptures that have bothered me. And those same Scriptures were, in part, what brought on the Protestant Reformation. Let me now share with you some of the passages that troubled him the most:

1) Habakkuk 2:4

"Behold, as for the proud one, His soul is not right within him; but the righteous will live by his faith."

2) Romans 1:16,17

"For I am not ashamed of the gospel, for it is the power of God for salvation to everyone who believes, to the Jew first and also to the Greek. For in it the righteousness of God is revealed from faith to faith; as it is written, 'But the righteous man shall live by faith.'"

3) Galatians 2:16
"Nevertheless knowing that a man is not justified by the works of the Law but through faith in Christ Jesus, even we have believed in Christ Jesus, that we may be justified by faith in Christ, and not by the works of the Law; since by the works of the Law shall no flesh be justified."

Martin Luther wrote, "Night and day I pondered until . . . I grasped the truth that the righteousness of God is that righteousness whereby, through grace and sheer mercy, He justifies us by faith."

The main text of this message is a companion passage to the one that bothered Luther. It is found in Galatians 3:10-14.

"For as many as are the works of the Law are under a curse; for it is written, 'Cursed is everyone who does not abide by all things written in the book of the Law, to perform them.' Now that no one is justified by the Law before God is evident; for, 'The righteous man shall live by faith.' However the Law is not of faith; on the contrary, 'He who practices them shall live by them.' Christ redeemed us from the curse of the Law, having become a curse for us—for it is written, 'Cursed is everyone who hangs on a tree'—in order that in Christ Jesus the blessings of Abraham might come to the Gentiles, so that we might receive the promise of the Spirit through faith" (Galatians 3:10-14).

One of the things that bothered me greatly when I was growing up was the concept of the judgment of God. Whenever I would do something wrong, my mother would point her finger at me and declare, with anger on her face, that someday I would stand before God and pay for all of my sins. It scared the 'hell' out of me! By age sixteen, I realized that I had already done so many things wrong that I could never do enough right things to make up for the wrong. I just gave up on the whole God thing and did my thing—the wrong thing. That is, I gave up until the day I heard the Scripture that says:

"Truly, truly, I say to you, he who hears My word, and believes Him who sent Me, has eternal life, and does not come into judgment, but has passed out of death into life" (John 5:24).

That one Bible verse changed my life. For the first time, I realized that there would be no judgment or condemnation for those who believe in Christ Jesus as Savior and Lord.

I believe people fall into three main categories. They are either: rebellious, religious, or righteous. How many of you are righteous?

Religious short-cuts always short-circuit our personal relationship with God. The Protestant Reformation dealt with this very issue. The Ninety-Five Theses posted on the side door of the Castle Church, in Wittenberg, Germany, on October 31, 1517, authored by Martin Luther, would change the Church forever. The problem was that the people had submitted to the authority of the Roman Catholic Church rather than the authority of the Holy Scriptures, and the authority of God. In so doing, they made God an abstract and mysterious being, rather than a personal loving God. And when God is not the central figure in the equation, you have no equation. When Jesus came to earth, He made His relationship with us personal. His jealousy for us brought Him here.

Living by the Law does not require faith. Man's attempt to live by the Law circumvents the gospel truth. Men *"suppress the truth by their wickedness" (Romans 1:18),* thereby incurring the wrath of God. Sin is man's obdurate attempt to encompass a different gospel. Desiring to view God as they choose they thereby stretch the mercy of God beyond acceptable limits. Anytime we talk about the things of God, we must be truthful, open, and aboveboard.

The Law itself is not redemptive, but is a means of clarifying and identifying sin. What the Law does, in effect, is increase sin: When the Law says don't, we do it anyway. Christ died to redeem us from the curse of the Law. Legalism is not redemptive. Legalism introduces people to the spirit of religion, because keeping religious practices is based on works, and works spring from pride and so mock God.

Proposition: Unraveling the tensions between lawlessness and legalism will set both the lawless and religious legalist free.

And there is this tension between the Law and religion and the church and what I can get away with and still not go to hell. So we make up our own rules that we think will be our excuse when we see God. But the Bible tells us that excuses won't cut it with God. "There is none righteous, no not one."

Legally Lost – the Curse of Lawlessness

"For as many as are the works of the Law are under a curse" (Galatians 3:10).

We must separate ourselves from the lawless. *"Do not be bound together with unbelievers; for what partnership have righteousness and lawlessness, or what fellowship has light with darkness? Or what harmony has Christ with Belial [a very wicked person], or what has a believer in common with an unbeliever? Or what agreement has the temple of God with idols? For we are the temple of the living God; just as God said, 'I will dwell in them and walk among them; and I will be their God, and they shall be My people. Therefore, come out from their midst and be separate,' says the Lord. 'And do not touch what is unclean; and I will welcome you. And I will be a father to you, and you shall be sons and daughters to Me,' says the Lord Almighty"* (2 Corinthians 6:14-18).

We are the "ekkaleo" (Greek) – called out from the world ones: *"A chosen race, a royal priesthood, a holy nation, a people for God's own possession"* (1 Peter 2:9a).

"Everyone who practices sin also practices lawlessness; and sin is lawlessness" (1 John 3:4).

The Law was established to protect the righteous and to punish the rebellious. *"But we know that the Law is good, if one uses it lawfully, realizing the fact that law is not made for righteous man, but for those who are lawless and rebellious, for the ungodly and sinners, for the unholy and profane, for those who kill their fathers or mothers, for murderers and immoral men and homosexuals and kidnappers and liars and perjurers, and whatever is contrary to sound teaching"* (1 Timothy 1:8-10). Another passage you may want to read on your own is: 2 Peter 2:1-8.

We must be careful to not assume that a person who appears to be spiritual and religious is saved. Jesus said, *"Many will say to Me on that day, 'Lord, Lord, did we not prophesy in Your name, and in Your name cast out demons, and in Your name perform many miracles?' And then I will declare to them, 'I never knew you; depart from Me, you who practice lawlessness'"* (Matthew 7:22,23).

Jesus, when He addressed the scribes and Pharisees called them hypocrites. He said they appeared clean on the outside, but inside they were full of robbery, self-indulgence, and lawlessness.

Lawless people will be condemned to hell. We must preach hell. Jesus preached more about hell than anyone else in the Bible. In fact, most of what we know about hell we learned from Jesus. We preach about hell because we don't want to see anyone go there. Listen to the words of Jesus:

"The Son of Man will send forth His angels, and they will gather out of His kingdom all stumbling blocks, and those who commit lawlessness, and will cast them into the furnace of fire; in that place there shall be weeping and gnashing of teeth" (Matthew 13:41,42).

Legally Lost – the Error of Legalism

"For as many as are of the works of the Law are under a curse; for it is written, 'Cursed is everyone who does not abide by all things written in the book of the Law, to perform them.' Now that no one is justified by the Law before God is evident; for, 'The righteous man shall live by faith.' However, the Law is not of faith; on the contrary, 'He who practices them shall live by them'" (Galatians 3:10-12).

Legalists are all condemned and under a curse, too. Legalism demands perfection—that's the Law. *"For whoever keeps the whole law and yet stumbles in one point, he has become guilty of all"* (James 2:10). Living by the Law does not require faith. We are saved by faith not by law. Abraham was a believer saved by faith before the Law.

Illustration:

Legalism is like getting poison oak (poison oak is a plant that grows in the wild that some people are allergic to): the more you scratch, the more you get. The more you come in contact with the poison, the more affected you become. I know a lady who was lost in the woods without water. Her survivalist training had taught her to find a wet space in a hill and insert a tube. By morning, water was pouring from the tube. Unfortunately, the tube was tapped into a poison oak root, resulting in a violent case of religious legalism. Do you get the point? There is a lot of tension between lawlessness and legalism. Can you feel the tension?

Legitimately Found – the Truth of Redemption

> *"Christ redeemed us from the curse of the Law, having become a curse for us—for it is written, 'Cursed is everyone who hangs on a tree—in order that in Christ Jesus the blessing of Abraham might come to the Gentiles, so that we might receive the promise of the Spirit through faith" (Galatians 3:13,14).*

Legally and legitimately, Christ broke the curse of the Law; that's the Law. Jesus became the perfect sacrifice. *"But with precious blood as of a lamb unblemished and spotless, the blood of Christ" (1 Peter 1:19).* Jesus accepted the condemnation for us all. He became the condemned man who bore our sins on the cross.

Legal and legitimate heirs to the promises given to Abraham are those who receive Christ by faith. The blessings of the generations and the breaking of all curses are accomplished through Christ. Jesus also broke the curse of death which means that no man needs to die anymore in his sins. For those who are in Christ Jesus never cease to exist. Yes, we all die. But when we die, (as believers) we just move from one state of earthly existence to another state of forever existence.

Legal heirs, Gentiles or Jews, receive the promise of the Holy Spirit. *"For all who are led by the Spirit of God, these are the sons of God. For you have not received a spirit of slavery leading to fear again, but you have received a spirit of adoption as sons by which we cry out, 'Abba! Father!' The Spirit Himself bears witness with our spirit that we are children of God" (Romans 8:14-16).*

The New Testament is a book about the Holy Spirit and man's journey with the Spirit. Everything we know about God comes from the spiritual realm. The word "SPIRIT" is used over four hundred times in the New Testament alone. To deny the movement of the Spirit is to deny the promises of God.

Educationally, intellectually, spiritually, and biblically, I know the things I have shared with you to be true. Yet, I know many Christians who have lived their whole lives in religious bondage, which I call the spirit of religion. I am talking about the ones who try to do all the right religious stuff, yet never feel they have quite measured up or fit into the religious box. It's kind of like keeping a coat in your closet that is too small. You hope some day you will lose all of that weight and fit back into it. You know you should give it away, but it is your favorite coat and you just can't part with it.

Religious bondage is like the water that was pouring out of the side of the hill that was tapped into the poison oak root. The water that was flowing out appeared to be clean and pure, yet the poison was polluting the water. That is what religious spirits do; they pollute the springs of living water.

The Promise of the Spirit Breaks the Yoke of Slavery

"It was for freedom that Christ set us free; therefore keep standing firm and do not be subject again to a yoke of slavery" (Galatians 5:1).

God lives in a realm where there is no darkness—no sin—total light. We would never be able to go there unless God could somehow blot out the sin in us. When the Spirit of God comes to reside in us, He breaks the yoke of slavery. Why then do we lose our freedom and find ourselves again in religious slavery?

"But it was because of false brethren who had sneaked in to spy out our liberty which we have in

Christ Jesus, in order to bring us into bondage" (Galatians 2:4).

"Now the Lord is Spirit; and where the Spirit of the Lord is, there is liberty" (2 Corinthians 3:17).

What then is the "yoke of slavery"? It is five things:

1) SIN: Sin steals our freedom and puts us under the bondage of the enemy. Jesus canceled and purged our sin from the record with His own blood. He blotted it out so that He could never see it again.

2) LAW: Living under the condemnation of the Law steals our freedom because we cannot keep the Law. Living under the Law puts us under the curse.

3) LEGALISM: Legalism cannot save you. We could never become good enough to stand before Holy God on our own human merit. Legalism is not freedom but slavery.

4) RELIGIOUS BONDAGE: The spirit of religion is the subtlest form of slavery and deception. Organizational sectarian Christianity can be a form of spiritual bondage. When serving a religious system takes priority over our relationship with God, we have been deceived. READ: Colossians 2:8-23

5) DEATH: The fear and chains of death are broken in Christ. Death is no longer an enemy, but a

conquered enemy. *"We are of good courage, I say, and prefer rather to be absent from the body and to be at home with the Lord" (2 Corinthians 5:8).*

I believe it is time to move away from sectarian and denominational Christianity.

The promise of the outpouring of the Holy Spirit was for the purpose of breaking the yoke of religious bondage.

"If you are led by the Spirit, you are not under the Law. Walk by the Spirit, and you will not carry out the desire of the flesh. If we live by the Spirit, let us also walk by the Spirit" (Galatians 5:18,16,25).

Free at Last – the Yoke is Broken

God wants us to be Spirit-directed, Spirit-driven, and spiritually discerning people. God wants to set people free from religious bondage. God is a jealous God who wants personal relationship with you through His Spirit. Jesus did not come to earth to give us a new religion, but SALVATION!

The fruit of the Spirit comes from the Holy Spirit. Man cannot produce the fruit of the Spirit, but the Holy Spirit in us produces the fruit. You cannot conjure up on your own God's kind of love or joy or peace or patience or kindness or goodness or faithfulness or gentleness or self-control. They are the blessings and rewards of walking in communion with God. He gives them to us liberally and without measure. God never called us to be fruit inspectors (of our tree or anyone else's). Enjoy the fruit He produces in you, for they are the blessings of life.

During the summer of 1998, Cheryl (my wife) had a real bad case of poison oak. After weeks of battling with topical ointments, it turned into hives. Eventually her throat began to swell. I rushed her in the middle of the night to the emergency room at the local hospital. The doctor treated her with intravenous antidote which helped her to overcome the affliction. In the same way, we need the medicine that comes only from the Holy Spirit, to set us free from the affliction of sin, the Law, legalism, and religious spiritual bondage.

Maybe you have been trying to wear a coat that is too tight. Perhaps you are frustrated because you have been unable to get the religion stuff just right. You love the Lord and you love the coat, but it just doesn't fit anymore. The coat represents the YOKE, and Christ has broken the yoke. You can be free! Free at last! Now get rid of the coat.

The springs of living water are flowing—out of your innermost being they flow to quench your thirst for God. The waters come from the well that will never run dry. They are the springs of eternal life. Jesus is saying to you here and now, "Come to the waters and be filled with the Spirit; come and be free at last." The springs of living water flush away the poisons that pollute our lives.

Warning! Do you remember the poison oak? Well, about six months later, my wife put on the shoes she was wearing the day she got the poison oak, and guess what—that's right, it came back again. The enemy will attempt to get you to return to the familiar religious spirits—but don't you do it, for you have been set free!

7

Religious Conflict

"Thus says the Lord God, 'Behold, I am against the shepherds, and I shall demand My sheep from them and make them cease from feeding sheep. So the shepherds will not feed themselves anymore, but I shall deliver My flock from their mouth, that they may not be food for them'" (Ezekiel 34:10).

It was one of those freezing cold winter days in the Black Forest area of Colorado, where I lived at the time. As usual on Saturday morning, we were about to have our weekly 6:00 a.m. men's prayer meeting. Our group of six men had been getting together for several months for breakfast, prayer, and chitchat; mostly breakfast and chitchat (small talk). Our prayer times always ended promptly at 7:00 a.m. This particular week, I was going through a hard time spiritually and really needed prayer for my circumstances. However, our prayer time usually lasted about ten or fifteen minutes, at which time we prayed for the President, the Congress, the poor kids in Africa, and so on. This Saturday, though, I would have none of it. I confronted each man in the group about their personal problems and asked why they had not asked for prayer. I then began to bear my heart, telling of my own need for prayer. I said, "If we cannot pray together as we should, I must leave the group."

That morning we began our prayer time at 7:00 a.m., and did not finish until after 9:00 a.m. There was not a dry eye in the group of six men. I believe most of those men had never cried since childhood, but that morning they wept bitterly and joyously before the Lord. We became, that day, intimately woven together by the power of the Holy Spirit. We never again had shallow prayer meetings.

Another interesting manifestation of the Spirit that morning was the sweat I found on my brow. It was a red watery substance that turned my handkerchief red. It was like the Holy Spirit was telling me: "This is it! This is the kind of fellowship I want My people to have." I quietly tucked the handkerchief away in my pocket without comment. I think it would have been too much for some of the men in our group to handle.

The great thing about this day, with these men, was that we received the meat of the Word through the power of Spirit. The meat of God's Word is much like the yoke of oxen and implements that Elisha the prophet sacrificed unto the Lord when he picked up the mantle of Elijah. For Elisha, it was an act of complete surrender in obedience. In the same way, we too need to capitulate to the sovereign will of the Father. This may mean that we will need to give Him our religious security blanket in order to receive the security that comes only from Him.

Lord, secure us now in Your love as we begin to deal with some of the perplexities of traditional Christian dogma, in light of kingdom living. Holy Spirit we pray for Your enlightenment. I know in my heart that many people want to see the power of God come into their situations and that He be exalted to the highest place. I don't believe this can happen, though, if one holds a view that is diametrically opposed to the Word of God. We cannot expect God to bless in His full power: error, rebellion, disobedience, or disloyalty. The golden thread that God has woven through His Word is—truth in love. When we won't receive the truth, we won't experience the love either. God's love seems boundless and endless, even for the vilest sinner. I pray you find the golden thread.

Is unity in the body of Christ a thing to be grasped? Is it possible? Jesus thought so. One time, at a prayer meeting with a group of pastors, I prayed for us to come into unity in the body of Christ. (By the way, the body of Christ is where two or more are gathered in His name.) Then, just two prayers later, a pastor thanked God for our denominational distinctives. God help us! He should have prayed that God would heal our dysfunction.

Paul wrote about unity and the building up of the body in faith to maturity. Then he states, *"We are no longer to be children, tossed here and there by waves, and carried about by every wind of doctrine, by the trickery of men, by craftiness in deceitful scheming" (Ephesians 4:14).*

The exceptions to unity should only be idol issues and immorality issues, as clearly stated in the word of God. The immorality issues should be obvious to all if you believe what the Bible says about these things. Idol issues are a different matter. Christian orthodoxy should be all that is needed to tutor us in our quest for unity.

Believers should move away from the "us" and "them" complex. The church is the work of the Holy Spirit. All work done by and through the Holy Spirit is His work. Everyone should also be careful to not make his denomination or organization his idol. "Idolatry is the paying of divine honors to any created thing, the ascription of divine power to natural agencies" (Unger's Bible Dictionary).

Some people are in love with the ministry or in love with their organization or in love with the "mores" of Christianity, but never experienced a personal relationship with Christ. They know the "genre," they know the "jargon," but they don't know the Savior.

Man's irresistible urge to control, manipulate, and overpower his fellow man is common in all cultures, whether they be political, economic, military, or religious. The fact of the matter is, no more that ten percent of the world's power base controls ninety percent of the people. The abuse of power usually causes division. And division causes these power structures to eventually fall apart. The Bible says to reject a divisive man after the first and second warning. Jesus said, *"Any kingdom divided against itself is laid waste; and a house divided against itself falls" (Luke 11:23).* In Christianity, these dynamics should not exist. In ministry one is called to "serve," not rule.

The natural desire for power is not compatible with the callings of God. Power and control issues are actually a violation of the biblical code of unity. The spirit of control and manipulation is what the Book of James calls jealousy and selfish ambition. James goes on to say that this wisdom is deception and not from God. He then says it is a lie against the truth. He also says the source of this kind of wisdom or power is earthly, natural and demonic.

Natural man uses earthly ways, natural gifts of leadership, and demonic influences to gain power, control, and money. These human influences have caused a great deal of mistrust among the common man.

The Church (the assembly of believers) has for centuries succumbed to the Roman order of rule. Western culture has adopted Western forms of government and applied those principles to Christ's Church. But is it biblical? For the past five centuries the rulers of the Western Church have basically adopted the hierarchical structure of the Roman Church. The Reformers reformed the theology, but not the church government.

And for the past five centuries the church rulers have tried to justify their positions of power, based on historical Christianity, legend, and tradition. We have accepted these cultural norms as biblical without question. For the past four hundred plus years, people known as Protestants have been trying to figure these things out, and the result has been more and more division or denominations. Each one of these groups claim their distinct views are right.

The discussion among the "clergy," during the era of John Calvin, was how the ruling clergy could control the people through theology. Whoever could come up with the right theology would be the group the people would follow. The catch phrase here is: "how to control the people."

It was not until the fourth century that the clergy class came into existence. Along with it came the mysteries of the unknowable God. Instead of Jesus becoming more personal to the believer, He became more mysterious and abstract. Enter religious ritualism and formalism: stained glass windows, high vaulted ceilings, steeples, religious garb, and ceremony. Soon the only people who could "know" God were the highly religious, and they became the "God-connection" for the people. This in turn gave rise to the sin of partiality. Let the Word of God now speak:

"My brothers, as believers in our glorious Lord Jesus Christ, don't show favoritism. Suppose a man comes

into your meeting wearing a gold ring and fine clothes, and a poor man in shabby clothes also comes in. If you show special attention to the man wearing fine clothes and say, 'Here's a good seat for you,' but say to the poor man, 'You stand there' or 'Sit on the floor by my feet,' have you not discriminated among yourselves and become judges with evil thoughts? Listen, my dear brothers: Has not God chosen those who are poor in the eyes of the world to be rich in faith and to inherit the kingdom he promised those who love him?" (James, 2:1-5) NIV

Unfortunately, we (the body of Christ) have had a very difficult time shedding ourselves of the sin of partiality. Any idea or philosophy that exalts and venerates one person over and above another breaks the spirit of unity in Christ's body. It is important for the common man to understand the quality of his own life and his valuable purpose in God's kingdom. When he does, it will set him free from religious partiality. God does not show personal favoritism or preferential treatment to anyone. Our accountability in the kingdom is not contingent on man's approval, but God's. So then, *"Work out your salvation with fear and trembling; for it is God who is at work in you, both to will and to work for His good pleasure"* (Philippians 2:12,13).

In the centuries before the Reformation, the clergy class, through ignorance and poverty, controlled a vast number of the God-fearing people. The benefactor of this approach was the Roman Catholic Church and its leadership. Jesus used the term "Benefactors" when referring to the status and position the disciples were seeking within their own ranks. Jesus said, *"The kings of the Gentiles lord it over them; and those who have authority over them are called 'Benefactors.' But not so with you, but let him who is greatest among you become as the youngest, and the leader as the servant"* (Luke 22:25,26). Then Jesus said, *"I am among you as the one who serves."* Religious "power posturing" has no place in the church.

I see three main inherent classical schisms within the institutional traditional Western Church, from which all other schisms develop:

1) Religious Ritualism: That branch of the Church that emphasizes the importance of the clerical priesthood, traditional rituals, importance of sacraments, and the formalism in style of worship.

2) Religious Formalism: That branch of the Church which sees a distinct separation between clergy and laity. They are deeply committed to doctrine, and see correct doctrinal beliefs as a way to salvation. Religious formalists are mildly committed to evangelizing the lost.

3) Religious Fundamentalism: That branch of the Church that is passionately evangelistic. They attach somewhat less importance to the clergy, laity caste

system, yet they still see the need for the established traditional structure. Fundamentalists are less concerned with doctrine, ritual, and form.

The problem with all these approaches is how God is viewed in light of these various perspectives. The institutional church has become the avenue, for many people, on how they see God, and what they believe about God.

One goes to the local church to worship God and to find comfort, direction, acceptance, and spiritual guidance. This approach is good for the seeker and the hurting. But stable and mature Christians should not go to church to get what they think they ought to receive. In other words, many people come to church with empty cups wanting to get filled up, and the church is guilty of propagating this myth.

I believe what Jesus had in mind when believers assemble is for them to come with filled cups, ready to empty out things such as: love and fellowship and encouragement and instruction and prophesy and revelation and psalms and hymns and spiritual gifts and financial gifts. What we should be doing is teaching people how to give away rather than receive. We need to find a way to teach people how to pour out God's love on each other with a servant's heart.

When one talks about the church, many people go from the objective to the subjective real fast. Immediately, we have a tendency to become defensive of our church denomination or historical position.

Discussing spiritual matters often requires a delicate approach. As we discuss some of these issues, I pray that you keep an open mind and heart. Try to remain objective. When one talks about the church, he always opens himself to much scrutinizing. Go ahead and scrutinize! Remember, we are not talking about your particular church, but the Church as a whole—all of Christendom.

The Roman Catholic Church holds the view that they are an infallible and a divinely inspired institution and thereby have authority over their members and their members have a divine obligation to that authority.

According to Protestant theory, churches are divine-human institutions they are not infallible. The rules of conduct must be in accordance with the teachings of the infallible Word.

Merrill F. Unger said, "The ethical standard of the visible Church must be simply that of the Holy Scriptures, otherwise the true idea of the Church is lost sight of and the Church assumes either too much or too little. Only by adhering to the Word of God as the 'rule of faith and practice' can the Church save themselves from the two extremes: on the one hand that of unduly magnifying authority of the visible Church or, on the other, that of laying aside its highest claim to recognition and obedience."

I think that the inhibition of maturation (lack of maturity) within the body of Christ may come from *arrogance* and *pride*. In other words, we can be so caught up in our own prideful opinions that we never grow up in Christ. We don't mature to the standard that Christ taught. Some are like the seeds, which fell among the thorns and are guilty of keeping the less mature in the thorns, in order to show superiority over them. In actuality, some feed off the immaturity seen in others, afraid to grow themselves. (Evil has been defined as the use of power to destroy the spiritual growth of another for the purpose of defending and preserving our own sick selves.)

A good understanding of basic traditional church terms will help us to find common ground.

CHURCH: Greek ekklesia (called out) assembly of believers – the body of Christ. Christian unity was answered in the out-pouring of the Holy Spirit at Pentecost, baptizing all who believe in Christ into one body into one Spirit. It is not organizational unity but the unity of a living organism. Christianity is not about doing church, but about each believer being the church.

DISCIPLE: Greek mathetes (learner) – the meaning is one who professes to have learned certain principles from another and maintains them on the other's authority. The term is applied principally to the followers of Jesus.

ELDER: Greek presbuterion (elder). The elders of the New Testament church were the pastors, bishops, overseers, teachers, and leaders. Peter, John, and Paul considered themselves fellow-elders, thereby showing equality with the other elders. There were no term limits for elders. When you became an elder, you remained an elder. It is conceivable that you could have a rather large body of elders within a particular church.

There also seems to be a plurality of responsibility assumed by those so deemed as elders, rather than some sort of hierarchical ruling structure, or ecclesiastical pecking order. The elders were to work together in various cities and towns with oneness or in unity.

The following Scriptures are the historical, traditional passages used throughout the history of the church as the basis for church government. Many of the verses following the passages have to do with the moral requirements for those who minister the Word.

Acts 20:17, 28
"... He sent to Ephesus and called to him elders of the church. 'Be on guard for yourselves and for all the flock, among which the Holy Spirit has made you overseers, to shepherd the church of God which He purchased with His own blood.'"

Notice the term "elders" in this passage is seen in the plural sense. Also notice how the terms elders and overseers are interchangeable.

Ephesians 4:11,12

"And He gave some as apostles, and some as prophets, and some as evangelists, and some as pastors and teachers, for the equipping of the saints for the work of service, to the building up of the body of Christ."

THE FIVE-FOLD MINISTRY

    1) Apostles – messengers sent on a mission
    2) Prophets – forthtellers
    3) Evangelists – bearers of good news
    4) Pastors – care and feed servants
    5) Teachers – instructors

Ephesians 4:13

"... until we all attain to the unity of the faith, and of the knowledge of the Son of God, to a mature man, to the measure of the stature which belongs to the fullness of Christ."

FOR THE PURPOSE OF:
    1) Equipping for service
    2) Building up the body of Christ – not division
    3) Until we attain to the unity of faith
    4) And attain a knowledge of the Son of God
    5) To a mature man
    6) To a measure, which is the fullness of Christ

7) So the body could be built up in truth and love.

REASONS FOR INSTRUCTION:
    1) To overcome ignorance
    2) Hardness of heart (callous)
    3) Sensuality & impurity
    4) Greediness
    5) Lusts of deceit
    6) Falsehood (apostasy)

Read: Ephesians 4:14-32 for amplification.

NOTE: This text does not seem to be an outline for church government. Rather it seems to be an exhortation to maturity and unity. It is about being built up together in love and unity through the use of spiritual gifts. This text is also the only place in the New Testament where the term "pastor" is used. It should also be noted that in the five-fold ministry there does not seem to be one of the spiritual functions that takes authority or precedence over the others.

1 Timothy 5:17
"*Let the elders [older men WHO TAKE THE LEAD –Greek] be considered worthy of double honor, especially those who work hard at preaching and teaching.*"

1 Timothy 3:1 (Greek NT literal translation)
"*Faithful the word: if any overseership stretches forward to of good work he is desirous.*"

NIV Translation: "Here is a trustworthy saying: if anyone sets his heart on being an overseer, he desires a noble task." (Best translation.)

Titus 1:5-9
"For this reason I left you in Crete, that you might set in order what remains, and appoint elders in every city as I directed you, namely, if any man be above reproach, the husband of one wife, having children who believe, not accused of dissipation or rebellion. For the overseer [ELDER], must be above reproach as God's steward, not self-willed, not quick-tempered, not addicted to wine, not pugnacious [quarrelsome], not fond of sordid gain, but hospitable, loving what is good, sensible, just, devout, self-controlled, holding fast the faithful word which is in accordance with the teaching, that he may be able to both exhort in sound doctrine and refute those who contradict."

NOTE: In this passage, the elder and overseer seem to be synonymous—equivalent in definition. Another interesting point that could be made is for the geographical appointment of elders. Christianity, during early times, was localized by, city, town, or village. The issues of church government do not seem to be obviously apparent within the New Testament framework. The gathering of elders to equip for service and evangelism does seem apparent. These three questions remain in my mind:

1) What if Christ never intended the church to become a formal institution?

2) What would the church look like without a hierarchical structure?

3) Has the church taken the form that Christ intended?

After examining the New Testament carefully, I am convinced that each local church should be responsible to God, for its own actions. Assuming that I am correct in this assumption, there would be no need for a religious hierarchy outside the local church. Neither would there be any division in the Church as a whole. In this context, each independent fellowship would be responsible to God for their actions. Let God judge each church on its own individual merit and sins.

The description of the requirements for those who minister seems to be more closely related to the integrity and morality of the individuals, rather than their authority and educational backgrounds. After all, most of the disciples Jesus chose were just fisherman. Maybe the Church needs more fisherman than scholars.

The main problem the Church faces today is to undo the hierarchal power structures. Any power structure (that is already in place) will rise up against anybody that attempts to threaten its power. This is why change is so difficult. This is especially true when you are talking about a large religious financial industry.

The New Testament abounds with warnings against false leadership. What if there were no central power or central government? Could the church survive? Or perhaps the better question is: Would the church thrive? Maybe the early church fathers believed that the church would never have such problems of division, especially in light of all the unity passages. Christ, along with the New Testament writers are in agreement that disunity and division is not a biblical option. We either accept our brother in Christ, or he is an anathema (accursed) and put out of the body. Agreeing to disagree is not optional. This sort of church discipline is not so feasible outside the local body. And that is why the local body is so important.

Differences are not a reason for division in the body of Christ either. If our differences are preventing the lost from being saved, we are in error. If how we do church business and church government is the reason for our division, why not let each body self determine those issues individually and according to the Scriptures. The major issue we should endeavor to flesh out is: How can we mobilize the masses to evangelize the lost to Christ? This too is best done on a local level.

Perhaps the major issue is not church government, church doctrine, or heresy, but position and pride. James Burns states in his book *The Laws of Revival*: "In religion, as in politics, there are two distinct camps, liberal and conservative. The watchword of the one is freedom, and the watchword of the other is authority. The conflict between the two is constant, but each represents too deep a factor of human life to destroy the other. Thus, a revival which carries to one extreme will be followed by a counter-movement in the other direction."

It is not so important where we have been as a Church, but where we are going. Perhaps many of the problems are rooted in the organizational structure of the Church, rather than the spiritual health and growth of the believer. I think it is time for Christians to become more spiritual and less organizational. It's time to again proclaim Christ and the cross and the resurrection and the life. It's time to set the people free!

When the people are set free, unity will happen. This is why I think it is time for a grassroots movement to come forth. Ecumenicalism originating from the clergy class has not brought greater unity to the body of Christ. If anything it has widened the rift between Christians.

When the common man (the ordinary Christian) refuses to be divided from his brothers and sisters in Christ, and will no longer embrace division and disunity as acceptable, then real unity will happen. Unity is best observed within a local body of believers. When the lost see our love and unity they will come to Christ—Jesus promised.

8

Trouble in River City

"Like a trampled spring and a polluted well; is a righteous man who gives way before the wicked" *(Proverbs 25:26).*

The problems in the church have become accepted as normal. People outside the church call it hypocrisy. We *good Christians* in the church approach our problems with a sense of self-righteous indignation. Notwithstanding, hypocrisy still remains. People outside the church see our lives, and if we are honest, we know they are right. We are hypocrites.

The liberalization of Christianity has called things the Bible declares as sin—as now okay. Does anyone have the right to override God's authority? Concession leads to corruption, but conviction of sin leads a man to holiness. *"Let God be true, and every man a liar"* *(Romans 3:4).*

Jesus said, *"Beware of the leaven of the Pharisees, which is hypocrisy"* *(Luke 12:1).*

We all know the enemy, Satan, is in the business of deception. Rick Joyner, in his book *The Call*, states: "Even the great Apostle Paul admitted to having been foiled by Satan. But don't be overly concerned about being deceived. That is actually one of his biggest traps. He sidetracks many by having them fear more in his power to deceive than to have faith in the power of the Holy Spirit to lead them into all truth. Those who have fallen into this trap not only fall into increasing bondage to fear, but they will attack anyone who walks in freedom that comes with faith. I am quite sure that you will not make it far up that mountain before they ambush you."

My prayer is: "Lord Jesus, help me to walk in freedom instead of fear."

The New Testament is loaded with warnings about religious deception. As believers walk the walk of the new covenant, they are exhorted to hold-on to sound doctrine and be fervent in the spirit. Christians are also encouraged to confess their sins to one another, and to live in peace and harmony. Additionally, the community of believers should judge and examine things carefully to see if it is from God. And to expose to the light the things that are in the darkness. When light dispels the darkness all fear is gone and freedom erases the shadows of doubt.

Jesus gave us warnings about apostasy, the misuse of power, and false authority. In the gospels are recorded thirty-three different confrontations Jesus had with the religious leaders of His day. A "woe" is a strong condemnation. The seven woes in Matthew 23:1-32, and the six woes on a different occasion in Luke 11:37-54, give us a view of some of the hypocrisy Jesus saw in the religious leaders. They are warnings against pretense, unreality in religion, ecclesiastical manipulation, pride, insincerity, shams, the misuse of power, and the misuse of religious traditions.

It is interesting that Jesus begins by rebuking the Pharisees for failing to recognize Him as the Messiah, and for holding back the kingdom of heaven from men. He accuses them of practicing religion under false pretense. He goes on to say their misguided zeal is doing more harm than good. Then He rebukes them for their misuse of the Scriptures and for their failure to discern the intent of the Word, which is justice, mercy, and faithfulness. He continues to tell them that they have been caught up in self-indulgences and robbery. He then calls them whitewashed tombs with the appearance of righteousness, yet full of lawlessness. He rebukes them for building memorials to the past, and for paying honor to those who killed the prophets. He then accuses them of paying the tithe, disregarding the justice of God, and of religious legalism.

Jesus went on to tell them that they loved the front seats in the synagogue and the respectful greetings in the marketplace. He rebukes them for their false pride and arrogance. He says that they weigh men down with heavy burdens, and at the same time do not lift a hand to help. In the final woe, Jesus accuses them of taking away the key of knowledge from the people for the purpose of control and manipulation, and yet still, not entering into His revelation themselves.

Jesus does not leave all the responsibility and blame with the leaders, but warns New Testament Christians to be on the alert concerning false teachers, leaders and prophets. The reason these issues are so important is because these various deceptions often counterfeit the gospel message, steal our freedom, ensnare us into falsehood, and attempt to control us through legalism and false religious practices. They substitute the work of the cross and the power of the resurrection for a different gospel.

Deception is often subtle and goes unnoticed by those being deceived. "If it sounds good it must be right!" Right? Unfortunately, many Christians have been deceived and are anesthetized by the subtle power of spiritual deception. Through keeping religious practices and rituals, they believe all will work out okay. The Scriptures are clear on these issues. Perhaps the delusion is a fulfillment of the passage in 2 Timothy 4:3: *"For the time will come when they will not endure sound doctrine; but wanting to have their ears tickled, they will accumulate for themselves teachers in accordance to their own desires."*

I have recorded several of these New Testament passages for your convenience. I thought it would be good for you to see the vast amount of Scripture on the subject.

Colossians 2:8-23

"See to it that no one takes you captive through philosophy and empty deception, according to the tradition of men, according to the elementary principles of the world, rather than according to Christ. For in Him all the fullness of the Deity dwells in bodily [human] form, and in Him you have been made complete, and He is the head over all rule and authority; and in Him you were also circumcised with a circumcision made without hands, in the removal of the body of the flesh by the circumcision of Christ; having been buried with Him in baptism, in which you were also raised up with Him through faith in the working of God, who raised Him from the dead. And when you were dead in your transgressions and the uncircumcision of your flesh, He made you alive together with Him, having forgiven all our transgressions, having canceled out the certificate of debt consisting of decrees against us and which was hostile to us; and He has taken it out of the way, having nailed it to the cross. When He had disarmed the rulers and authorities, He made public display of them, having triumphed over them through Him.

Therefore let no one act as your judge in regard to food or drink or respect to a festival or a new moon or a Sabbath day—things which are a mere shadow of what is to come; but the substance belongs to Christ. Let no one keep defrauding you of your prize by delighting in self-abasement and the worship of the angels, taking his stand on visions he has seen, inflated *without cause by his fleshly mind, and not holding fast to the head, from whom the entire body, being supplied and held together by the joints and ligaments, grows with a growth which is from God. If you have died with Christ to the elementary principles of the world, why, as if you were living in the world, do you submit yourself to decrees, such as, 'Do not handle, do not taste, do not touch!' (all of which refer to the things destined to perish with using) in accordance with the commandment and teachings of men? These are matters which have, to be sure, the appearance of wisdom in self-made religion and self-abasement and severe treatment of the body, but are of no value against fleshly indulgence."*

Jude 18, 19, 16
"'In the last time there shall be mockers, following after their own ungodly lusts.' These are the ones who cause divisions, worldly-minded, devoid of the Spirit. These are grumblers, finding fault, following after their own lusts; they speak arrogantly, flattering people for the sake of gaining an advantage."

2 Peter 2:1-3a
The entire second chapter deals with the issues of deception. *"But false prophets also arose among the people, just as there will also be false teachers among you, who will secretly introduce destructive heresies, even denying the Master who bought them, bringing swift destruction upon themselves. And many will follow their sensuality, and because of them the way*

of the truth will be maligned; and in their greed they will exploit you with false words."

2 Peter 2:17-19
"These are springs without water, and mists driven by a storm, for whom the black darkness has been reserved. For speaking out arrogant words of vanity they entice by fleshly desires, by sensuality, those who barely escape from the ones who live in error, promising them freedom while they themselves are slaves of corruption; for by what a man is overcome, by this he is enslaved."

Philippians 1:15-17; 3:2; 3:18,19
"Some, to be sure, are preaching Christ even from envy and strife, but some also from good will; the latter do it out of love, knowing that I am appointed for the defense of the gospel; the former proclaim Christ out of selfish ambition, rather than from pure motives."

"Beware of the dogs, beware of the evil workers, beware of the false circumcision, . . ."

"For many walk, of whom I often told you, and now tell you even weeping, that they are enemies of the cross of Christ, whose end is destruction, whose god is their appetite, and whose glory is their shame, who set their minds on earthly things."

Ephesians 4:14

"We are no longer to be children, tossed here and there by waves, and carried about by every wind of doctrine, by the trickery of men, by craftiness in deceitful scheming."

2 Timothy 3:1-13 (selected)

This is a prophetic word for the end times concerning the deception of the masses and the various characteristics of those doing the deceiving and those being deceived. There are eighteen vices listed that emphasize the condition of the people:

"But realize this, that in the last days, difficult times will come. For men will be lovers of self, lovers of money, boastful, arrogant, revelers, disobedient to parents, ungrateful, unholy, unloving, irreconcilable, malicious gossips, without self-control, brutal, haters of good, treacherous, reckless, conceited, lovers of pleasure rather than lovers of God; [HOLDING TO A FORM OF GODLINESS, ALTHOUGH THEY HAVE DENIED ITS POWER]; and avoid such men as these. For among them are those who enter into households and captivate weak women weighed down with sins, led on by various impulses, always learning and never able to come to the knowledge of the truth. But evil men and impostors will proceed from bad to worse, deceiving and being deceived."

Galatians 1:6-10; 2:4

"I am amazed that you are so quickly deserting Him who called you by the grace of Christ, for a different

gospel; which is really not another; only there are some who are disturbing you, and want to distort the gospel of Christ. But even though we, or an angel from heaven, should preach to you a gospel contrary to that which we have preached to you, let him be accursed. As we have said before, so I say again now, if any man is preaching to you a gospel contrary to that which you received, let him be [Greek anathema] *accursed. For am I now seeking the favor of men, or of God? Or am I striving to please men? If I were still trying to please men, I would not be a bond-servant of Christ. But it was because of false brethren who had sneaked in to spy out our liberty which we have in Christ Jesus, in order to bring us into bondage."*

Listed below are several other portions of Scripture that deal with the issues of false leadership:
  2 Timothy 3:1-13
  2 Corinthians 11:13 & 26
  1 John 4:1-6
  Titus 1:10-16
  James 3:13-18
  2 John 7-11

If we live in constant fear of deception the enemy has won, because fear and not faith is in control. If we live without fear of deception we are being foolish. Pray that the Lord will protect you from the evil one and deliver you from evil and deceptive forces. Pray that God will give you discernment. I think that one of the hardest things for anyone to admit is that they have been deceived. Many stay in cults and religious sects even when they know there is deception. Maybe it is because they are unwilling to admit the truth. Or perhaps it is because they know that if they leave, it will cost them their associations, friends, and family. Jesus said, *"A man's enemies will be the members of his household. He who loves father or mother more than Me is not worthy of Me; and he who loves son or daughter more than Me is not worthy of Me. He who has found his life shall lose it, and he who has lost his life for My sake shall find it"* (Matthew 10:36-39).

God is a God of new beginnings. Don't be afraid to fight for what is right. *"Like a trampled spring and polluted well; is a righteous man who gives way before the wicked" (Proverbs 25:26).* Truth is love.

9

The Journey of Life in the Kingdom

"He who has My commandments and keeps them, he it is who loves Me; and he who loves Me shall be loved by My Father, and I will love him, and I will disclose Myself to him" (John 14:21).

God truly is a God of new beginnings. Many of us have failed to meet His expectations and struggle with the past. We all flounder at times, as a lost soul, to understand and incorporate into our daily lives certain unchangeable requirements for intimacy with God. We instinctively know our striving is against the spiritual forces of darkness. But why do we resist His wooing, His Loving arms, and His security? Maybe we too want to be god. Then we wrestle with the truth about ourselves and know our limitations. Perhaps if we honestly and consciously can keep our contradictions in clear view, we will be able to overcome.

Here then are some of the contradictions that limit our freedom and security in God:
1) His will versus our defiance
2) Walking by faith versus self-reliant independence
3) Trust versus mistrust
4) Faithfulness versus defection
5) Revelation versus obedience to the revelation
6) Unity versus isolation
7) Sabbath rest and time with God versus my own agenda.

One thing that will break the spirit of unity in the body of Christ faster than any other is the spirit of arrogance and self-will. Arrogance is the opposite of humility and brokenness. Revival will come when men put away themselves and exalt Christ to the highest place. Arrogance will erode the foundation of communion with the Spirit and with the saints. When man exalts himself, he brings God down to his level, and the Spirit departs. Christians must be willing to put their backs to man and their faces toward God.

It's all about Him. Some people live and die for causes, and others die *just because*. Christians live because Christ lives in them and to die is gain. I have seen the arrogance of man and am guilty of it myself for which I repent of here and now. Arrogance is of the flesh and flesh and blood does not inherit the kingdom. *"For the mind set on the flesh is death, but the mind set on the Spirit is life and peace"* *(Romans 8:6).*

In his *Book of Prophecies*, published until recently only in Spanish, Christopher Columbus wrote:

"It was the Lord who put it into my mind (I could feel His hand upon me) the fact that it would be possible to sail from here to the Indies. All who heard of my project rejected it with laughter, ridiculing me. There is no question that the inspiration was from the Holy Spirit, because He comforted me with rays of marvelous inspiration from the Holy Scripture. I am a most unworthy sinner, but I have cried out to the Lord for grace and mercy and they have covered me completely. I have found the sweetest consolation since I made it my whole purpose to enjoy His marvelous presence. For the execution of the journey to the Indies, I did not make use of intelligence, mathematics, or maps. It is simply the fulfillment of what Isaiah prophesied. 'No one should fear to undertake any task in the name of our Savior, if it is just and if the intention is purely for His holy service.' Our Lord has assigned the working out of all things to each person, but it all happens according to His sovereign will, even though He gives advice. He lacks nothing that it is in the power of men to give Him. Oh, what a gracious Lord, who desires that people should perform for Him those things for which He holds Himself responsible! Day and night, moment by moment, everyone should express their most devoted gratitude to Him."

"It was the Lord who put it into my mind." In the same way God spoke to Columbus, He wants to speak to you. He has a divine plan and you are a part of His plan. Indeed, what message does God have for His servants? Maybe He just wants us to be a servant. It's not about our power; it's about God's power working through a submitted servant.

What great exploits does the Holy Spirit have for you to do?

Exploits are acts of brilliance or heroic feats that one can utilize to become productive. When you get hurt, shake it off and say to yourself: "These are just the brandmarks of Jesus and I wear them proudly."   If your foundation has slipped away, build a new one with safe people. Or have you become so inflexible that you won't obey anyway? Do you really want a personal relationship with Christ? Or do you just want it your own way? Are you going to choose to remain hurt and offended?

"Many are called, but few are chosen" (Matthew 22: 14).

"And the Lamb will overcome them, because He is Lord of lords and King of kings, and those who are with Him are the called and chosen and faithful" (Revelation 17:14).

If you are one of the called—faithful—chosen, there must not be negotiation with the devil on this point. If you are chosen, God has not changed His mind nor rejected you. If He has called and chosen you, He has not changed His mind on that point either. And if you are called and chosen, remaining faithful is not negotiable.

Several years ago I had an experience in the Lord that was unique to say the least. I share it with you so you will understand the importance of remaining faithful.

I'll never forget that day. All the feelings of a lifetime seemed to have merged—that day—that memorable day in September when my dad, the family patriarch, died. When I arrived at the hospital, family members took me to a room where the lifeless body of my father lay on a gurney, waiting transport to the local funeral home. I was overcome with grief and emptiness. I wept. No one could know the loss I felt because the loss was personal and known only to me. He was part of me and I him; he was my dad, my example, my mentor, and my friend. He was always bigger than life to me; setting standards for life no man could live in the shadow of. He was a man large in stature with hair as white as snow. He was quiet, gentle, and loving, yet strong, conservative, and resilient. When he walked into a room, his presence commanded the respect of everyone.

The last time I saw my dad alive was just six weeks before his death. He looked tired and older, the lines of age were deeper, and his usual gait was gone; yet he still had a contagious enthusiasm and zest for life. I knew down deep we needed to spend quality time together, and so we did. I took time off work and we played, for the first time, just like two childhood pals. We went golfing. On the following day we drove to the High Sierra Mountains of California to camp and fish.

The summer days of August (1990) were hot and hazy as we drove from the valley floor. The high country was just what we expected: clean, cool, and refreshing. The aspens shimmered in the gentle breeze. The lakes were full of trout and there was still snow on the glaciers. My dad loved the wild flowers: daisies, crocuses, and beautiful purple iris that were in the meadows and around the lakes and streams.

Dad had a fondness for fishing. I think it was one of the things he dreamed about all those years he labored ten to twelve hours a day, six days a week, on his job. He was never a great trout fisherman, yet on this trip he caught more fish than I, an unusual event. We sat at night around the campfire and just talked. How I needed that time with him! We slept side by side in the back of my old van, a seventy-five year old dad and a forty-six year old son. This was the only time I can remember spending more than just a few hours alone with him. He was a private man who rarely talked about himself. He possessed a quiet resolve about life found in few men—his trust was in the Lord, and his strength came from deep within.

I think, because of my rebellious years growing up and my hyperactivity as a child, that he never liked me very much. I knew he always loved me, yet I also knew that I never quite measured up to his expectations of the ideal son. It was not until the last few years before his death that I earned his respect. The four days and three nights we spent together on the camping trip were the finest ones we ever had. We solidified our relationship as father and son, affirming and loving each other. These final days were ordered and ordained by the Lord and have become God's greatest blessing to me. As I stood in the hospital room, the flashback of this trip helped me deal with my pain and the details of his home going.

Three days after his burial (for only a few seconds), I saw my dad again but in a glorified state. He was young, radiant, and happy. His words to me were, "It's all real, it's wonderful, and it's worth it—remain faithful!" And then he was gone as quickly as he appeared.

I live everyday with those words ringing in my head —remain faithful, remain faithful. You are a chosen servant, a royal priesthood, a person of God's possession, and you must remain faithful.

Along with remaining faithful, one must also keep his guard up against the spirit of offense. It is important for you to know that the spirit of offense is not from God. The enemy has used this tactic to destroy many Christians. Jesus came to bind up the brokenhearted and set the captive free. *"For you have not received the spirit of slavery leading to fear again, but you have received the spirit of adoption as sons by which we cry out, 'Abba! Father!'" (Romans 8:15).*

Perhaps you are one who has been hurt by someone in the religious system, and maybe you have been hurt several times. You don't need to just stand there and take it. Move on, shake the dust from your feet, keep your eyes on Jesus, and find a safe group of people to fellowship with. If the spirit of fear and offense has kept you in slavery, break the chains because the chains are not from God.

There are some good people out there who have broken fellowship with other Christians. Some have left the Church because of the issues of unity and liberty. Others have left because of hurt feelings, and still others have left because of spiritual abuse by a leader. Here's the word for you—God has not granted you a certificate of divorce from His Church. To divorce yourself from Christ's Church is a violation of the truth you proclaimed when you accepted Him as Savior.

When I read through the New Testament, I see no arrogance or pride in Jesus or the disciples. Miracles were happening all over the place and no doubt they were filled with joy and excitement, but not arrogance. Maybe it was because of the things Jesus had taught His disciples like, *"Blessed are the gentle, for they shall inherit the earth. Blessed are the merciful, for they shall receive mercy. Blessed are the pure in heart, for they shall see God. Blessed are those who hunger and thirst for righteousness, for they shall be satisfied. Beware of practicing your righteousness before men to be noticed by them; otherwise you have no reward with your Father who is in heaven" (Matthew 5:5,7,8, 6; 6:1).*

One night, while writing this book, I had a dream. In this particular dream I was the overseer of a farming project. There were many laborers who worked on this farm. The picture I saw was of a field of rich black soil that appeared ready to plant. It had been plowed and disked; all it needed was the furrows and for the seed to be planted. There were several bags of seed stacked ready for this purpose.

The field was surrounded by hills and forest. Everything appeared to be lush and green, but there arose a problem with the water supply. The spring that had supplied the field with water for centuries had dried up. I felt overwhelmed by the problem until the owner of the field showed up and directed me to hire a core drilling crew to come and drill into the field to determine if there was any water available deep under the field.

I remember feeling very responsible for all the workers standing around doing nothing while this process was going on. I felt that the time to plant was now and that we could not wait much longer.

One of the things I remember about these days was the beautiful contrast between the deep blue sky, the rich black field, and the lush green surroundings. There was also another unusual feature that entered into the picture—a beautiful white dove that just kept flying around the situation. Occasionally it would hover over me; it had a calming effect on my agitated condition over the dilemma regarding the water and the field.

As the drilling went on day after day, I became more and more anxious about the problem. Occasionally the owner of the field would show up to check the progress. He was never anxious or worried about the dilemma, but seemed to have a quiet resolve about the process we were in. I might also add that his presence had a soothing effect on my jumbled nerves.

Just when I thought we were making good progress, another problem developed—the core drillers had struck a vein of pure gold. What were we to do now? I had hoped this new find would not be a deterrent to our goal of finding water.

About that time the owner of the field showed up and made the decision to blow up the field in order to extract the precious gold. My mind simply would not compute this idea. The field was my responsibility; I had prepared it for planting and felt compelled to complete my task. But the owner of the field would not have it. He said it is his field and his decision. About that time the dove appeared and seemed to be saying to me that everything would be okay if we would just listen to the landowner. The owner of the field assured me that all the workers would share in the proceeds of the gold.

The last thing I remember about the dream was the explosion of the field. There was mud, dirt, and rocks flying everywhere. The workers were running around covered in dirt and mud with joyful expressions on their faces.

It was then I woke up and tried to understand the meaning of the dream. The whole experience was very unusual for me because I seldom remember anything I dream.

During the course of the dream I got the feeling that the field represented the program-driven, institutional church; the field also represented the ways of the world. The unplanted seed represented the unsaved souls of men. The landowner was God and the dove represented the Holy Spirit. I felt that to the land owner, finding the gold was more important than planting the field. The workers in the field represented the true and faithful Christians. I believe the gold represents the relationship Christ wants to have with His people. Gold is also a symbol of the kingdom. The field is God's problem not man's; He owns the field and He gives the increase.

Jesus said, *"No one can come to Me, unless the Father who sent Me draws him" (John 6:44).* The water represents the promise of Jesus. *"If any man's thirsty, let him come to Me and drink. He who believes in Me, as the Scripture said, 'From his innermost being shall flow rivers of living water'"(John 7:37,38).* The blowing-up of the field means that God desires relationship more than ritual, traditions, program, and structure. The drilling process was a description of God wanting man to go deep with Him, past the layers and layers of history and legends of man.

For me it became a relief to no longer need to worry about the field, because now I was living in the kingdom. There was also this great sense of joy I felt in my relationship with my fellow workers as we shared the benefits of the kingdom.

God is a God of milestones, not millstones. *"Thus the heavens and the earth were completed in all their vast array. By the seventh day God had finished the work he had been doing; so on the seventh day he rested from all his work. And God blessed the seventh day and made it holy, because on it he rested from all the work of creating that he had done. This is the account of the heavens and the earth when they were created. When the LORD God made the earth and the heavens...." (Genesis 2:1-4). NIV*

Even God had a stopping place, a time of rest. The time of rest was also part of God's creation. It is as real to Him as the elements of the Universe, in fact, it is His final act of creation, His crowning moment. It would be the time when all creation would come and prostrate themselves at His feet and worship Him for all that He has done. A time set aside for man to delight in God and a time for God to delight in man. If we do not enter into the Sabbath rest we will not experience peace with God.

"Therefore, let us fear lest, while a promise remains of entering His rest, any one of you should seem to have come short of it. There remains therefore a Sabbath rest for the people of God.

"Since therefore, brethren, we have confidence to enter the holy place by the blood of Jesus, by a new and living way which He inaugurated for us through the veil, that is, His flesh, and since we have a great priest over the house of God, let us draw near with a sincere heart in full assurance of faith having our hearts sprinkled clean from an evil conscience and our bodies washed pure with water.

"Let us hold fast the confession of our hope without wavering, for He who promised is faithful; and let us consider how to stimulate one another to love and good deeds, not forsaking our own assembling together, as is the habit of some, but encouraging one another; and all the more, as you see the day drawing near" (Hebrews 4:1,9; 10:19-25).

The rest God wants us to enter into is the field where the blessings are.

Most of us suffer in our relationship with God from neglect, not intellect. We neglect the thing we need the most—time with God. Our theology may be right and our motives wrong.

Intelligence and reason and intellect is not a relationship. Our relationship with God forms the basis for our stability. We become unstable when our relationship with Him is unstable. When we are unstable, we lose our confidence. Stability is not achieved through program or the millstone of our labors. Our stability is found in the Sabbath rest with the Father. It's not about doing for the kingdom, but living in the kingdom. When we are unstable ourselves, it becomes difficult to proclaim the kingdom in all its power.

"The LORD is exalted, for he dwells on high; he will fill Zion with justice and righteousness. He will be the sure foundation for your times, a rich store of salvation and wisdom and knowledge; the fear of the LORD is the key to this treasure" (Isaiah 33:5,6). NIV

To trust God is to fear God. People that fear Him in the negative sense don't know or trust Him. When He is God in your life, stability happens. When we feel secure in a stable relationship with God, we will experience the rest and freedom He wants us to enjoy as well. The security I am talking about has nothing to do with earthly possessions and finance. When we are secure in our relationship with Him, we feel secure in His provision. God does supply all your needs according to His riches in glory when you trust in His provision and are living without compromise in His will and purpose.

Kingdom living is realized through submission, not permission. God will allow you to do your own thing through His permissive will, but even that would be considered rebellion. When you are doing your own thing, you are limiting God's blessings. It's kind of like shooting yourself in the foot.

There is a certain amount of stability we can find when we are in relationship with God's people as well. We all have needs for affection, affirmation, and affiliation. These things are important parts in building the kingdom, because, as you are building up others, you are being built up as well.

God is a God of order and regularity. That's why He wants you to set aside regular time with Him and regular time with His children. That's what the early Christians did:

"They devoted themselves to the apostles' teaching and to the fellowship, to the breaking of bread and to prayer. Everyone was filled with awe, and many wonders and miraculous signs were done by the apostles. All the believers were together and had everything in common. Selling their possessions and goods, they gave to anyone as he had need. Every day they continued to meet together in the temple courts. They broke bread in their homes and ate together with glad and sincere hearts, praising God and enjoying the favor of all the people. And the Lord added to their number daily those who were being saved" (Acts 2:42-47). NIV

First Century Christians were not program, organization, or distinctive dependent. They were Holy Spirit dependent. Their righteousness, peace, and joy came from the love relationship they had for Jesus and the fellowship they had with each other. When someone tried to stand up and take ownership of what God was doing, the Apostles would step in and declare: "It's not about us, it's about Jesus!" Those early Christians set an example for us to follow, but we aren't following His example as we should.

When believers understand the freedom they do have in Jesus, they will become like the Christians of those first few centuries who went everywhere proclaiming the kingdom of God to everyone. And when people live in the kingdom, they can't keep quiet about the kingdom. Sadly, only a small amount of Christians ever share Jesus with someone in their lifetime. When people become free in Christ they will proclaim the kingdom of God from the housetops.

The power Jesus promised (the baptism in the Holy Spirit) at Pentecost was for the purpose of releasing His power into us to enable us to become witnesses for Him. This precious gift was not given for the purpose of self-edification. If people have received the Holy Spirit and are not witnessing to others they are misusing the gift and the anointing. Unity with other believers is perhaps the strongest weapon we possess against the enemy. Jesus, in His prayer recorded in John 17, said that people would come to Him when they saw the unity in us. (Author's paraphrase.)

Unity respects each man's right to individual Christian liberty as long as his liberty does not result in bondage for another.

Perhaps one of the most difficult things the early disciples faced was accepting, embracing, and adopting people who were not of their own racial, national, or cultural group. We tend to take this miraculous feat for granted. To the Jew, Gentiles were dogs. To the Jew, the Romans were the hated oppressors.

Many of us are taught to be proud of our ethnic and religious backgrounds, after all, they represent our heritage . . . right? Heritage is no more than traditions you inherited, if in fact, you can truly inherit such things. The early disciples understood the importance of having a holy alliance only with Christ. The only thing true Christians can inherit is the kingdom of God, and the blessings that come as a result of living in Christ's kingdom.

God created each human to be different and unique. Then when Jesus came, He set down a new requirement that exhorts us to find a way to take our uniqueness and unite it with others, to form His Body the Church. He did not ask us to go and find others that share our uniqueness—to fellowship with. It is our diversity and uniqueness that is needed to bring vitality to the Church.

"The God who made the world and everything in it is the Lord of heaven and earth and does not live in temples built by hands. And he is not served by human hands, as if he needed anything, because he himself gives all men life and breath and everything else. From one man he made every nation of men, that they should inhabit the whole earth; and he determined the times set for them and the exact places where they should live. God did this so that men would seek him and perhaps reach out for him and find him, though he is not far from each one of us. 'For in him we live and move and have our being'" (Acts 17:24-28). NIV

As we bring to an end the contradictions in our lives, we will be able to walk with joy and liberty in the gifts and callings of God. Defiance and self-will now set aside, we begin to get a fresh vision for the future.

Things that were out of focus before have become clear. God has indeed brought new life to our journey.

10

The Goat and the Tire

"Trust in the Lord, and do good; dwell in the land and cultivate faithfulness" (Psalm 37:3).

If there was one thing my father taught me, it was to be faithful to go to church every Sunday; something I have done my entire Christian life. One particular Sunday my wife had decided to stay home and do some things the Lord had been directing her to do. For the past year I had been visiting various denominations to better understand and evaluate the different worship styles and the distinctiveness of different denominations. This specific Sunday I was in a church with worship style and tradition I was familiar with.

It was early in the service when I began to feel something that made me shudder. I felt a strange spiritual presence, something I had felt at other times in religious settings. I asked the Lord what was going on. His question to me was, "What are you doing here? Did I send you here?" Startled by this, I did not know what to do, so I just got up and left (something I had done only one other time).

On the way home the Lord began to reveal to me that it was a "religious spirit." He directed me to take a certain route home so He could show me something. Not far from home I began to listen and watch more and more closely. Then I saw it—it was a goat chained to a tire. "That's it!" I felt the Lord say. "This is what the religious spirit is like; it's like a goat chained to a tire." The goat had certain freedoms, but his freedom was limited. When I arrived home, I related this experience to my wife, Cheryl.

Here, in her own words, was her reaction: "That morning I went into my quiet place and cried out to God, 'Can't I be a goat chained to the tire if I want to be! Isn't that one of my choices?'

"It took months and months to process what manner of freedom Christ was offering. I began to watch that goat on various trips past the property. The goat had many choices. She could sit on the tire, stand with front legs up higher than hind legs, turn around, walk in circles, and wander until she ran out of chain. She always seemed to be so content in her circumstances. And yet, she was and still is chained to the tire!

"The Lord began revealing my personal relationship with the institutional church. For over thirty years we've had one favored place of worship until a move or circumstance separated us from "our church." We often went early and stayed late for services and events. The church was the center of our world as we raised our three daughters.

"It seemed strange that during our thirty-second year of marriage, God was challenging us to look deeper at the motivation and reason for our various church involvements.

"He was asking me questions like, 'Did I ask you to go to the altar and pray for that person? Why did you pat that grieving person's shoulder? Why did you give money to that indigent person in the parking lot? Why did so many *I shoulds* motivate your week? Did I send you to this service? Did I ask you to invite that person?' He is teaching us about situational Christianity, duty bound by *I shoulds*. In other words, we in America respond in certain ways to the Western cultural norms. Has our culture led us into the freedom that Christ died for? Are we as a body of believers where the church was eighteen hundred years ago? What is the Lord telling us about a new freedom for today? Why is He calling us to listen so carefully to His still small voice? What if His voice begins to call us from our perfected box-like faith? What if we are to respond as He leads, rather than to simply react to our former cultural conditioning?

"In my past church life, I felt 'safe.' Yet, I understood the spoken and the unspoken rules. I knew what was expected of me in my role as a nurturer, exhorter, and prayer warrior. But was I free to move as Christ directed? Was I free to experience the unknown path of following the whisper of God's voice? Or...was it easier to follow the clamor of expectations? Did I simply follow the path of least resistance? Have the legends of man gotten in the way of restoration, renewal and revival? And what am I going to do about it?

"Those were painful months of *religious detoxification*. But God will raise up a powerful work of His Spirit if we will just listen to His still small voice. His choice for us is no more chains."

Religious Spirits

The problem with religious spirits is that most of us have them without knowing it. Religious spirits usually come as a result of practicing religion before man. Jesus said, *"Beware of practicing your righteousness before men to be noticed by them; otherwise you have no reward with your Father who is in heaven"* (Matthew 6:1).

This was a problem Jesus spoke to often because the bondage in it is self-idolatry. The id or the need for instant gratification or acceptance is an impulse one should avoid. When practicing religion puts you on the throne instead of Christ, you probably have a religious spirit. Many of the Pharisees and rulers did not have a problem intellectually believing in Jesus. Their problem was self-idolatry.

"Nevertheless many even of the rulers believed in Him, but because of the Pharisees they were not confessing Him, lest they should be put out of the synagogue; for they loved the approval of men rather than the approval of God" (John 12:42,43).

Our value in the kingdom is neither contingent nor dependent on the approval of men, but in the righteousness of Christ. He alone is our righteousness, our defense, our rear guard, and our salvation.

All many people want is to be normal, as if normal is their life-long goal. What is it to be normal? Jesus does not expect us to be normal, but extraordinary. Not mundane, but committed and passionate. God's plan for you is anything but normal. Normal is being lukewarm. Are you sure you want to be normal?

Jesus said, *"Enter by the narrow gate. Many will say to Me on that day, Lord, Lord, did we not prophesy in Your name, and in Your name cast out demons, and in your name perform many miracles? And I will declare to them I never knew you. But seek first His kingdom and His righteousness"* (Matthew 7:13,22,23; 6:33).

Our righteousness is about what Christ has done and not about what we do. He makes us righteous through His blood and not our works. It's called "Amazing Grace, how sweet the sound."

Self-idolatry is the darkness of the religious spirit. Jesus called all men everywhere to be salt and light. If you are full of light, your light will dispel the darkness, but be careful to not let your light cast dark shadows. Darkness does not comprehend light. In fact the deeds of darkness hide from the light, fearing exposure. Light loves light. Be the light. Truth is the source of light and humility is a kissing cousin.

God has a plan for each person, a Divine assignment. The church should be a safe place where each believer has opportunity to carry out that assignment. If God wants us ALL to be in ministry, who and what is holding us back? Seeing people set free to do the work and ministry that God has called them to do is one of the reasons for writing this book.

God is now calling to His people to go deep after the things of the Spirit, and to go forth in His power. We must restore the ardor and zeal of mercy and compassion that was evident in the early church. People need to be set free to do Christ's work as He leads. If all we do is work to serve a program, an organization, or tradition, we're limiting God. If God wants us to be in relationship with Him more than anything else, and if He has sent the Holy Spirit to be our guide and helper, why don't we spend more time listening to Him instead of doing religious activities?

Why do we feel so limited to do the things the Spirit is telling us to do? When God says, "Do not let routine command your thinking," then it's time to break loose and walk in obedience to God rather than man.

When God leads you to do a certain work—go do it. You don't need to check in with man to see if it is okay. It is, I think, the fear of man that is holding back the kingdom of God from man. When man begins to fear God more than he does man, God will be praised.

We tell people about Christ's kingdom because we

are "kingdom kids." Christianity was not supposed to become a religious campaign for a certain program, political agenda, or movement.

Jesus wants it to be a camp-out where He puts fish on the coals and has breakfast with you. You are just as capable of following the leading of the Spirit as anyone else. When you are true and faithful to Christ and His Word, then you can do what He says you can do. Jesus wants to break your chains of dependence on rituals and tradition. He wants to set you free. He wants to pull you through the eye of the needle to the other side. Jesus wants you dependent on Him and Him alone.

Christianity is based on a personal relationship with Him. He has set you free! *"If therefore the Son shall make you free, you shall be free indeed" (John 8:36).*

I believe there is a spiritual darkness that has laid over the church for centuries, and I believe it is the blanket of the religious spirit(s). God is pulling the blanket off and offering a new freedom. He wants to be your covering, and the covering is liberty, peace, and joy in the Holy Spirit. The question is "Do you want His covering?" Are you ready to throw away your security blanket and walk with courage and trust in the King of kings?

We must return to the pre-Constantine era and condition of the church. We must again embrace Christian orthodoxy that is rooted in "correct doctrine" and "right praise." (Correct doctrine—that is opposed to all sects and heresies, and right praise—that is in the spirit of love and humility.) We must all again become an integral part of the whole.

This perspective is no kin to the Universalism perspective, which attempts to amalgamate apostasy with orthodoxy.

"God is Spirit, and those who worship Him must worship in spirit and truth" (John 4:24). This double emphasis, spirit and truth, defines the importance of accuracy and intent.

I agree with the statement made by Martin Luther: "I believe there is on earth a certain community of saints, composed solely of holy persons, under one Head, collected together by the Spirit; of one faith, and one mind, endowed with manifold gifts, but united in love, and without sects and divisions."

The power of the gospel is the freedom we have in Christ. Why the deception? Why hide the truth of Christ's message under ritualism and non-biblical tradition? Why hold to a form of godliness and deny the power of the message? What is it we, the religious, are trying to protect the people from?

Why the mystery? Why are we trying to make Jesus so mysterious? Why does the church not grow as it did in the first three centuries? Maybe it is because we have surrendered our Christian liberties. The proclamation of the gospel should not only be our first priority, but our personal responsibility. Let your light shine and don't expect someone else to shine it for you.

"You were formerly darkness, but now you are the light in the Lord; walk as children of the light (for the fruit of the light consists in all goodness and righteousness and truth) trying to learn what is pleasing to the Lord. And do not participate in the unfruitful deeds of darkness, but instead even expose them; for it is disgraceful even to speak of the things which are done by them in secret. But all things become visible when they are exposed to the light, for everything that becomes visible is light" (Ephesians 5: 8-13).

We, as the church, have become so accustomed to the darkness that we are afraid to confront it. It's like we are trying to protect the evil we know that exists, rather than exposing it to the light. Why are we trying to protect false brethren? If the disciples were willing to contend for the faith, why aren't we?

"Therefore, laying aside falsehood, speak truth, each one of you with his neighbor, for we are all members of one another" (Ephesians 4:25).

When I was twenty years old, I decided I wanted to learn how to be a cook. So I went to the best restaurant in our town and asked the head chef for a job. He hired me as a dishwasher. Then he promised that he would teach me all he could about cooking. After several months, he encouraged me to quit my job as a dishwasher and seek a job as a cook.

He warned me that I might be fired a few times before I could hold a cooking job, but eventually I would learn enough to keep one. I learned by trial and failure. From that time on, I was never "qualified" for anything, but willing to do everything. Yes, willingness and fortitude became my ally. In a very short time, I found myself cooking at some of the finest restaurants in our area.

When it comes to ministry, many people feel insecure and unqualified. Just imagine how those Galilean fishermen felt those first days of ministry. No doubt they were filled with fear and apprehension. But they had just received the power of the Holy Spirit to become witnesses, and they were. The rulers and the scribes were amazed and dumbfounded by their abilities. They did (as promised) stand before kings, governments, and rulers for the sake of Jesus. The Holy Spirit filled their mouths with words the rulers could not refute. They did not walk in fear of man but in the fear of God.

Contend for the faith, brothers and sisters—contend for the faith! More specifically, contend for your faith.

11

The Kingdom of Love

"He has brought me to His banquet hall, and His banner over me is love" (Song of Solomon 2:4).

While I was in my study one morning, I received a call from some Christian friends. They felt the Lord was telling them to anoint Humboldt County (the area where we live in California) with oil to break the strongholds of the enemy.

They had a definite route, procedure, and plan for this endeavor. They set forth the same procedure King David used when he moved the Ark of the Covenant to Jerusalem. In 2 Samuel 6:12-15, the Ark was returned from the house of Obed-Edom to the City of David with rejoicing, shouting, dancing, and the sound of the trumpet. Every six steps they sacrificed a bull and a fatted calf.

Six represents the number of man and what we can do in our own strength. Our sacrifice was to put down our own reasoning and rely solely on the Lord's leading. Every six miles on the journey we stopped to see what the Lord would reveal to us at that point. There was to be no idle talk between the six mile marks, only prayer, music played from CD's in their car, and some Scripture reading as the Lord led.

My friend rigged his car to run a steady stream of virgin olive oil down through the steering column.

It was early spring and the day was cold and rainy; but we saw this, too, as a test of our faith and obedience. From the very outset it was obvious to us all that God was in it with us. He had a plan and we were doing His plan. The trip lasted over four hours as we circled the county. At some places, we sang praises and waved flags. Other times we just listened and watched for signs from the Lord.

I think the main thing we all sensed was the awesome power of God in the car that day. At our second stop, we were out in the country in front of a farmhouse that was set quite a distance back from the road. There I found some very fragrant wild roses, which I picked to take along with us. Cheryl picked some wild flowers that looked like lily-of-the-valley; they too became part of our journey. As we continued, I wondered what it all meant. I kept meditating: "Rose of Sharon, Rose of Sharon."

At the next stop, we were in the middle of the forest. As I looked around I saw a wild apple tree in bloom. I went to it and picked some of the blossoms, and added them to our collection.

As we started out again, I grabbed my Bible and opened it to the Song of Solomon, chapter two. It reads as follows: *"I am the rose of Sharon, the lily of the valley." "Like a lily among the thorns, so is my darling among the maidens." "Like an apple tree among the trees of the forest, so is my beloved among the young men. In his shade I took great delight and sat down, and his fruit was sweet to my taste. He has brought me to his banquet hall, and his banner over me is love"* (Song of Solomon 2:1-4).

What the Lord wanted to show us on our journey that day was here in these few verses. It is, in fact, the greatest revelation of all. It is the revelation of His profound and overwhelming love. God was delighted by our obedience and willingness to do the unusual and different as a sacrifice of praise to Him. The car was filled with His fragrance and presence. I can't describe the joy and love we felt in those moments. Every stop from there on was a revelation of His love. He set the table and we partook in His presence.

We anointed the Humboldt County with several gallons of pure olive oil, and He anointed us with His Holy Spirit. This, I believe, is what living in the kingdom is all about. This was the revelation.

What God is doing in these days is raising up a remnant in His Church who have remained faithful and true to the Word of God. Now is the time to listen very carefully to the leading of the Holy Spirit. Walk in His leading without resistance, even if you don't completely understand with your mind. Find your purpose in God and just go with it. Remember that God is the biological Father of us all, and that we are all products of His creation. His plan for us is everlasting life. That everlasting life begins now.

When we realize that what we do now, with Jesus, has eternal dimensions, our perspective of the kingdom will escalate to new heights. We must understand that God is both our Father and our friend. When we follow His leading, our hearts will soar in response to His unfolding love. Intimacy with Him is His desire for us.

"Thine eyes have seen my unformed substance; and in Thy book they were all written, the days that were ordained for me, when as yet there was not one of them" (Psalm 139:16). "That which is born of the flesh is flesh, and that which is born of the Spirit is spirit. Unless one is born again, he cannot see the kingdom of God" (John 3:6,3).

Jesus is the promised and prophesied everlasting Father of us all. *"For a child will be born to us, a son will be given to us; and the government will rest on His shoulders; and His name will be called Wonderful Counselor, Mighty God, Eternal Father, Prince of Peace" (Isaiah 9:6).*

When we accept Him, He accepts us. We become, through adoption, His sons and daughters—children of God.

"But when the fulness of the time came, God sent forth His Son, born of a woman, born under the Law, in order that He might redeem those who were under the Law, that we might receive the adoption as sons. And because you are sons, God has sent forth the Spirit of His Son into our hearts crying, 'Abba! Father!' Therefore you are no longer a slave, but a son; and if a son, then an heir through God" (Galatians 4:4-7).

"For you have not received a spirit of slavery [SIN] leading to fear again, but you have received a spirit of adoption as sons by which we cry out, 'Abba! Father!' The Spirit Himself bears witness with our spirit that we are children of God. For all who are being led by the Spirit of God, these are sons of God" (Romans 8: 15,16,14).

"For the kingdom of God is not a matter of eating and drinking, but of righteousness, peace, and joy in the Holy Spirit" (Romans 14:17). NIV

In order for us to better understand our Father's heart (concerning His expectations of us), we will do well to understand the kingdom perspectives. In the Gospel of Matthew, chapter thirteen, we find the parables Jesus told concerning kingdom living. As we look at each parable we should consider how each one relates to our own agenda.

The following parable of the sower has to do with the attitudes and pure motives of the heart:

"Then he told them many things in parables, saying: 'A farmer went out to sow his seed. As he was scattering the seed, some fell along the path, and the birds came and ate it up. Some fell on rocky places, where it did not have much soil. It sprang up quickly, because the soil was shallow. But when the sun came up, the plants were scorched, and they withered because they had no root. Other seed fell among thorns, which grew up and choked the plants. Still other seed fell on good soil, where it produced a crop - a hundred, sixty or thirty times what was sown. He who has ears, let him hear.'

"The disciples came to him and asked, 'Why do you speak to the people in parables?' He replied, 'The knowledge of the secrets of the kingdom of heaven has been given to you, but not to them. Whoever has will be given more, and he will have an abundance. Whoever does not have, even what he has will be taken from him. This is why I speak to them in parables: Though seeing, they do not see; though hearing, they do not hear or understand. In them is fulfilled the prophecy of Isaiah: 'You will be ever hearing but never understanding; you will be ever seeing but never perceiving. For this people's heart has become calloused; they hardly hear with their ears, and they have closed their eyes. Otherwise they might see with their eyes, hear with their ears, understand with their hearts and turn, and I would heal them.' But blessed are your eyes because they see, and your ears

because they hear. For I tell you the truth, many prophets and righteous men longed to see what you see but did not see it, and to hear what you hear but did not hear it" (Matthew 13:3-17).

Kingdom living is truth and trust in our relationship with God. Kingdom living is abiding in the revelation of God and the mysteries of His kingdom. God speaks to us in revelations; we respond in obedience to the revelations. Kingdom living is doing the Father's will.

If God speaks His will to you and you choose to not obey, why would He reveal the next step to you? Many miss the kingdom because they will not receive the kingdom. Kingdom living requires personal responsibility and accountability. Kingdom people are blessed because they hear, see, and perceive with their heart. It is not my kingdom, but His kingdom. His kingdom come, His will be done—not my kingdom come and my will be done.

"And He was saying, 'The kingdom of God is like a man who cast seed upon the soil; and goes to bed at night and gets up by the day, and the seed sprouts up and grows—how, he himself does not know. The soil produces crops by itself; first the blade, then the head, then the mature grain in the head. But when the crop permits, he immediately puts in the sickle, because the harvest has come'" (Mark 4:26-29).

We must always be careful to not minimize another man's work. The growth of the kingdom is not always observable. Oftentimes it is God's unseen work in the hearts of men. Some of you have already been *in motion* for many years and have not yet seen the harvest of your labors. But, I tell you in advance, the harvest is coming—do not grow weary. God is at work doing both the visible and the invisible. To those who understand, these are the mysteries of the kingdom. Therefore, as you sow your seed, and as God speaks revelation to you, He will give you your assignment. And then He will release you, in freedom, to do His work.

The assignment God has for you to do may be the hardest and most difficult thing you have ever done. It is your test. When you pass the test, get ready for the next one. Because God sees in you much, much more than you will ever be able to see in yourself. He will push you along (with His hand on your back), and you will accomplish feats you never thought possible. Some will scoff at you, others will mock, and others will be jealous of your courage. Do God's assignment. Do the works of righteousness.

Christopher Columbus said, "Nothing that results from human progress is achieved with unanimous consent and those that are enlightened before the others are condemned to pursue that light in spite of others." Many of us today are like Columbus, embarking on a journey where we cannot see the outcome, or where it will take us. The passion for truth and freedom in Christ must sustain us through the persecution that most certainly will befall us.

The parable of the tares and the wheat deals with the heart condition of the person, in relationship to good works. Only time will tell the results of each man's work. The church is not perfect. There are weeds among the wheat. God will deal with the weeds in due time.

The parable of the mustard seed is about our faith in relationship to the kingdom. Faith grows from faith to faith. You either live in a little kingdom or a big kingdom. Extensive growth is visible growth. Do not compare yourself with others; not all plants grow at the same rate.

The parable of the leaven is about our invisible growth in the kingdom. Yeast brings about intensive internal transformation in the inner man. Yeast grows from small beginnings. Yeast produces substance and sustenance.

The parables of the hidden treasure and the pearl of great price are much like the dream the Lord gave me about the field. It's about the things you value most and about whom you value most. It's about your heart's condition toward God in relationship to living in His kingdom.

In the final parable, Jesus talks about the net that has been cast into the sea: *"Again, the kingdom of heaven is like a dragnet cast into the sea, and gathering fish of every kind; and when it was filled, they drew it up on the beach; and they sat down, and gathered the good fish into containers, but the bad they threw away. So it will be at the end of the age; the angels shall come forth, and take out the wicked from among the righteous, and will cast them into the furnace of fire; there shall be weeping and gnashing of teeth. 'Have you understood all these things?' They said to Him, 'Yes.' And He said to them, 'Therefore every scribe who has become a disciple of the kingdom of heaven is like a head of a household, who brings forth out of his treasure things new and old'"* (Matthew 13:47-52).

Jesus brings us to a point of circumspect self-analysis of how we view ourselves in relationship to kingdom living. There are many who want to get into the kingdom, but don't want to live in the kingdom now. The new things and the old things are the revelations about His kingdom that God reveals to us as we grow in Him. We grow through His Word from revelation to revelation.

When God reveals to you truth about His kingdom, you are responsible for that truth. Personally, I feel duty bound to proclaim that truth, lest I be found guilty of subverting the kingdom by the sin of omission.

Jesus said, *"For where your treasure is, there will be your heart also"* (Matthew 6:21).

Living in the kingdom now is like getting a down payment on your inheritance.

The Kingdom of Love

The Hebrew word "love" means to boil, to be on fire, to have affection and unity. It is the pot of gold that one finds when he/she is in union with Jesus. The Messiah's love is a constant love that refines us by fire and tempers us by the gentle soft touch of His Spirit.

Bedrock gold is the gospel of peace, joy, liberty, unity, charity, and praise in the Lord Jesus Christ. It is singing the song of love with affection and passion. Here is how John the Apostle defined love: *"This is how we know what love is: Jesus Christ laid down his life for us. And we ought to lay down our lives for our brothers" (1 John 3:16). NIV*

John is not talking about a social gospel that is defined by *ought to, should have, could have*, and *guilt* directed toward the unsaved world. What he is addressing is how we ought to treat our brothers and sisters who are already in Christ. Unfortunately, our zeal for evangelism is often misdirected and misguided away from the body of believers. We have become more *seeker sensitive* than believer sensitive.

When we are spiritually unhealthy on the inside, our message becomes a stumbling block to the unsaved world. As we serve one another in love, our love will become evident to all.

During my many years of jail ministry, I was always troubled with where to send the men after they got saved and released from prison. Where could they go and feel accepted? Most of them have already experienced a lifetime of rejection. Acceptance, affirmation, affiliation, and affection are what they really need. To tell the truth, that is what I really need, and I think it is what you really need, too.

Our Christian environment must be a place where the ground has been plowed and fertilized with the essential elements of the Holy Spirit. Otherwise our religion is worthless. We have spent too much time and effort detailing the doctrine and church government, and too little time on the essentials.

If we, as Christians, begin to agree on the broader context and majors of Christianity, and decide to leave the expression of the minors to individual understanding and conviction, we will do well. In so doing, we will achieve unity with clarity and liberty in diversity. Accountability will come to each one individually when they stand before the throne of God.

We are not responsible for another's interpretation or perception of biblical truth, unless it departs from historical Christian orthodoxy. It is, however, each person's responsibility to speak the truth about Christ in love. The expression of Christ's love takes on many creative forms and disciplines. We must respect each one's right to those expressions, and still walk in love and blessing.

It takes a lot of time, material, money, and energy to build a wall or fence. Each person must take down the walls that exist in his/her own heart in order to represent Jesus in a way that's relevant to a lost world. Arrogance, pride, and the unseen powers of darkness

The Kingdom of Love

are all that is holding back the greatest outpouring of the Holy Spirit the world has ever seen.

Now is the time for peace and unity among the brethren. Not walls. Not war. Each believer must begin to speak peace and love to the brethren. "And the greatest of these is love."

"Now to Him who is able to keep you from stumbling, and to make you stand in the presence of His glory blameless with great joy, to the only God our Savior, through Jesus Christ our Lord, be glory, majesty, dominion and authority, before all time and now and forever. Amen" (Jude 24,25).

"The righteous man shall live by faith" (Galatians 3:11). YES, THE RIGHTEOUS MAN DOES LIVE BY FAITH!

MY LEGACY

I dedicate this book to my three daughters: Lishelle, Deena and Tammy. I write it to them as my legacy of my faith in God. I pray that they will in turn pass it on to their children. May the phrase, "remain faithful" forever ring in their ears, for it is my father's legacy to me.